Advance Praise for *Part*

"Writers, you've got a new BFF—Deb Norton
what she says; you will not have writer's blo...
—Ellen Sandler, former coexecutive producer and writer, *Everybody Loves Raymond*, and author of *The TV Writer's Workbook*

"Deb Norton's *Part Wild* provides insightful tools to unleash your writing's full potential and unlock the infamous writer's block."
—Marisha Mukerjee, writer, *The Bridge*, *Heroes Reborn*, and *Quantico*

"*Part Wild* is like having a personal writing coach at your disposal twenty-four hours a day. Stuck, blocked, or in hiding, you're guaranteed to be freed by something in this volume from the fear that binds and suppresses your best impulses. It will transform you from the writer you wish you were to the writer you've always known you could be."
—Lyn Greene, coexecutive producer, *Masters of Sex*, and executive producer, *Boss*, *Nip/Tuck*, and *The Interestings*

"Resistance is a natural part of the creative process. It is the tension that births new life. I am so grateful to Deb Norton for her brilliant work with resistance; she has helped to transform the complexities of the creative process into functional, effective practices . . . that work! *Part Wild* is more than a book on creative writing, it is an essential guide for creative living."
—Dara Marks, PhD, author of *Inside Story: The Power of the Transformational Arc*

"This is a wise, delightful, and powerful book, unlike anything else of its kind I've come across. It's written by a writer for writers, and you can feel that compassion and rigor on every page. Norton shares practical ideas with grace and ample lashings of humor. Writers of all kinds will find this a godsend."
—Ellen McLaughlin, playwright, actor, and professor of playwriting, Barnard College

"Deb Norton's writing is infused with so much heart and compassion, and her unique sense of humor and curiosity are infectious! This book inspired me to PLUNGE!"
—Didi Conn, actress and playwright

"When you get stuck in your writing—and I'd give a 99.9 percent for-sure guarantee that you will—take hope. Somewhere in *Part Wild* you will find just the right suggestion to get you moving. Deb Norton is the highest-leaping cheerleader a writer could wish for!"
—Nina R ... nder, *Utne Re*... arms

A WRITER'S GUIDE TO HARNESSING THE CREATIVE POWER OF RESISTANCE

DEB NORTON

ATRIA
ENLIVEN BOOKS
New York London Toronto Sydney New Delhi

Enliven Books
An Imprint of Simon & Schuster, Inc.
1230 Avenue of the Americas
New York, NY 10020

First Enliven trade paperback edition September 2016

This publication contains the opinions and ideas of its author. It is intended to provide helpful and informative material on the subjects addressed in the publication. It is sold with the understanding that the author and publisher are not engaged in rendering medical, health, or any other kind of personal professional services in the book. The reader should consult his or her medical, health, or other competent professional before adopting any of the suggestions in this book or drawing inferences from it.

The author and publisher specifically disclaim all responsibility for any liability, loss, or risk, personal or otherwise, that is incurred as a consequence, directly or indirectly, of the use and application of any of the contents of this book.

Interior design by Renato Stanisic

Manufactured in the United States of America

10 9 8 7 6 5 4 3 2 1

Library of Congress Cataloging-in-Publication Data is available.

ISBN 978-1-5011-2915-5
ISBN 978-1-5011-2916-2 (ebook)

Part Wild is dedicated to my husband, Chris,
without whom I would never have known I was a teacher.

Preface

I got the title of this book from my dog, Al, a smart, sensitive, mostly well-behaved Queensland heeler mix who was my constant companion for fourteen of her sixteen years. Al had some truly inexplicable behaviors and habits that no amount of training or socializing could alter. For instance, Al "sang" loudly in the car whenever I took a route she didn't approve of or put the car in fourth gear. It was a dead-on imitation of Yoko Ono at the height of frenzy, and there was no getting her to stop. If I held her muzzle closed, she sang inside her mouth. She also barked at the sun and moon, was rude and snobby to other dogs, didn't like her sides to be touched, and absolutely would not stand for anyone taking her picture. Then, as if these weren't enough quirks for any dog, Al developed a new habit. After walking off leash her whole life, she began to stray from my side and stroll into our rural road to stand in front of oncoming cars. I told her this was absolutely forbidden, but she wouldn't hear it. I started leashing her for our walks, and she was not pleased.

When I discovered that one of the writers in my workshop was a pet psychic, I thought, *What the heck, maybe she can speak to Al and find out what on earth made her want to walk into the road.*

Laura sat down next to Al, and they put their heads together conspiratorially. After just a few moments, she looked over at me, laughing. "I'm sorry; it's really not funny," she said. "I told her she has to stop going into the street and she said, 'But the people in the cars like to see me. It makes them happy.'"

I would never have guessed this reason for Al's behavior. "But she's going to stop, right?"

"Yes, I told her if she wants to be off leash, she has to do what you say."

"Good. What about all the rest of it? The singing and the barking."

"Oh, Al says she can't help it because she's part wild."

"Excuse me?"

Laura looked at Al as if for confirmation. "Yep. Part wild. And she says she wants a kitty." She looked at Al again. "And a duck."

Al never did stray into the road again after speaking with Laura. I let the rest of it go. As long as her behaviors were merely eccentric and not dangerous, why try to tame them out of her? The duck, though—that was a bridge too far.

In a world that rewards conformity and compliance, it can be a challenge to stay in touch with our wild instincts. Al was a great, well-behaved dog when she wasn't giving me a heart attack by "letting people see her." She was the living embodiment of a balanced, part tame/part wild nature. Instead of stripping the oddness out of her, I started watching her for tips on how to get my own tame and wild parts to play nicer together, especially when it came to the creative process, where they were often very much at odds.

Introduction

All humans come preloaded with a wild creative spark that wants to be expressed in the writing of songs or the throwing of pots or the invention of new technology. How else would we have evolved as a species if we didn't possess an innate urge to create something new, to innovate, and to explore? Isn't that what creativity is—the natural desire to transcend the known and become greater than the sum of our parts? By hardwiring us with these creative desires, nature gave us—fangless, clawless, and slow as we are—a huge leg up on survival.

There's a reason inspiration feels so good, and it's the same reason sex does. Pleasure encourages us to procreate and to create. In both cases, when the urge is denied, life becomes downright uncomfortable. And when creation takes hold, whether in the form of new life or a new idea, the birthing can be arduous. Think of it this way: just as the pain of childbirth can only be relieved by having a baby, the pain caused by the urge to create can only be relieved by creating. Unlike childbirth, however, which is widely seen as a natural and worthwhile endeavor, our creative instincts often meet with an array of forces of resistance ranging from denigration to procrastination.

It's a wonder that anyone, anywhere can get creative work made, but artists and writers do find a way. The trick, I'm convinced, is to harness the power of the resistance rather than fight it.

I've worked with writers and artists at all points on the creative trajectory, from never-put-pen-to-paper to peak-of-profession-and-paralyzed, and I've seen firsthand that when the impulse to create receives support and direction, miracles really do occur. In addition to something new and wonderful being made in the world, relationship problems resolve, depression lifts, self-destructive behaviors abate. People even become more physically robust. Right before my eyes, this has happened time and again when my clients learn to push off of resistance and use this momentum to unleash their creative energy.

In other words, resistance is not necessarily the enemy of creativity, any more than gravity is the enemy of walking. Resistance is not good or bad—it just is. What matters is how you work with it.

The wild part of our nature urges us to explore and create something new that will elevate our existence and possibly the existences of others, but this drive must run the gauntlet of the wiring that perceives our creative impulses to be dangerous. Our tame side resists our desire to explore unknown territory because it might be full of predators, poisonous insects, quicksand, and goodness knows what else. Creative impulses promote daydreaming and distraction, which make us sitting ducks for the twenty kinds of death that could befall us from above, below, and behind. There's also the fact that our wild creativity can make us seem a little strange, and nonconformity threatens our place in the tribe. Before they are recognized as mavericks, artists, healers, and leaders, many creative people are first identified as . . . weirdos.

So dealing with resistance means accepting both sides of our primal nature, the one that wants us to be safe and sound and the other that wants us to go out on a limb and make something spectacular. Every one of us has to figure out how to be a productive and socially acceptable tribe member who can also "go rogue" and engage in some free-range self-expression—like Al with her car singing.

This is not easy to do—at least it wasn't easy for me.

In the tiny and very conservative oil town in the California desert where I grew up, everything was sand-colored, including the people. There was no art, no record store, no coffee shop; the radio offered either country music or church.

Stories saved me, prying my little world open and nourishing my imagination. I loved stories: reading them, seeing them, hearing them, telling them; personal, historical, lyrical, fantasy-fictional or science-fantastical. I loved them so much that I wanted to be a part of telling them, so I tried out for school plays, in which I got to explore my full range of weird wildness, playing every role from Lizzie Borden to a Norwegian mother of six, all before the age of fifteen.

I followed this path straight into a graduate acting program. There, I got to step inside stories written by all my heroes. For three years I was hot-dipped in Chekhov, Tennessee Williams, Caryl Churchill, and Oscar Wilde. I got to be a part of telling important, political, epic, ancient, musical, moving human stories. It was challenging and fulfilling and thrilling. And then . . . I graduated.

Only a few years into my acting career, I became frustrated by the endless professional junk that superseded the work: agents, auditions, showcases, on-camera workshops, networking, competing, branding and packaging myself to stand out. There was too much "No" and not enough "Go." I had known all this was part of the job, but when it got down to it, I just wasn't cut out for the hustle.

The few times I did get the "Go," it was usually for a story that I didn't passionately care to tell. What I wanted was to give people that pry-you-open-insert-meaning experience, the kind of experience that had lifted me up so many times, given me the juice to keep going and to keep my heart open. And I didn't like having to beg and bang down doors to get to do something that felt so imperative.

And then my friend Nancy suggested to me that you didn't have to audition to pick up a pen and write. The mere thought of this kind of freedom sent anxiety pumping through my nervous system. Nancy was correct, of course; there was nothing to stop me from writing the story I wanted to perform in—except my own inner critic, who was quick to impress upon me that I would never write like Edward Albee or Suzan-Lori Parks. Never in a million years. So why even try?

Somehow, Nancy managed to coax me into doing "just some little exercises." When I sat down to write purposefully that first time, I was drenched in flop sweat before I'd filled half a page of the legal pad she'd lent me. Every word had to be dragged, kicking and screaming, through a strafing of shockingly cruel inner criticism and self-doubt, but when we stopped writing and read our scribblings to each other, there was something there: Ideas. Bits of characters. Starts of stories. When I took those starts away and tried, on my own, to develop them further, my inner critic hammered me. There were no agents, no auditions, no room full of twenty-five people vying for the one minor part—there was only me and two of the most powerful tools known to humans, pen and paper, and I was still full of "No."

Maybe it was a matter of educating myself, I reasoned. If I understood the writing process better, I'd be less freaked out by it. So I turned to my most trusted resource, books. I read books on writing and the creative process, books about writers, and writers' memoirs—and everything I read just made me feel more overwhelmed and more filled with dread. The books advised being original, authentic, raw, and truthful. No pressure! They admonished that a strong, fresh voice was key, but they didn't reveal how one's voice could be found or even where to start looking for it. They stressed the importance of discipline and grit—neither of which was any kind of match for my fear. What I really needed, more than anything, was a book that would help me understand why the process was so fraught, why my own internal resistance was getting the better of me.

And then I found it! *The War of Art*, by Steven Pressfield, named every single kind of resistance I'd ever experienced, and then named some more. It was like a taxonomy of creative terrors. It was so liberating to find that these struggles had a name, and that I wasn't the only one who experienced them.

Now I had the name, rank, and serial number of every soldier in the enemy's army, but I still didn't know how to fight back. In fact, just the thought of fighting made me want to build a bunker and seal myself in, because . . . I'm just not a fighter. I mean, I should probably have taken a clue from the title of Pressfield's book, but if I were the type to put up my dukes and take on resistance, wouldn't I have done it already? Initially, understanding the enemy set me back even further.

So I demoted writing to a hobby and started a mosaic business. I cut sheets of glass into little squares and painstakingly glued them all over every floor, wall, tabletop, candleholder, window, and flowerpot in my path. I opened a gallery, taught classes, and made the world a prettier place for several years.

Meanwhile, the writing that I had safely contained to hobby status was conspiring to become a fully written play. Scenes nudged at me and dialogue pushed into my head as I cut and glued and grouted. Despite all my efforts to keep it in a hidden little corner, the play began elbowing its way to the front of my mind. This story wanted to be told, and the more I held it off, the sharper its elbows got.

Damn it, I thought. *Why can't I just make stuff? Why does it have to be this whole big conflict?* I wanted to write but I didn't want the "war" that came with it, because my resistance was legion. I couldn't shake the Lord of the Rings–style vision in my head, in which an endless, teeming army of goblins poured over a hill, laying waste to everything so that nothing could ever grow there again. In that scenario, I was never reaching for my sword—I was running away.

Finally, I did what I should have done to begin with: I looked up the word *resistance*. The first and second definitions were what I expected: opposition, the ability to withstand attack, etc. But the third definition took me completely by surprise:

> **3. ELECTRICITY.**
> a. Also called **ohmic resistance:** a property of a conductor by virtue of which the passage of current is opposed, causing electric energy to be transformed into heat: equal to the voltage across the conductor divided by the current flowing in the conductor: usually measured in ohms. **Abbreviation:** R.
> b. a conductor or coil offering such opposition; resistor.

Fighting resistance felt futile because it *was* futile, like fighting electricity. You can't win, and besides, there are better things to do with electricity—like plug in to it and use it to power up.

I began to see how resistance created a special kind of heat whenever I got near rich and risky material. Instead of fearing this heat, I let it warm my process. I found I could use the tension resistance offered to slingshot me into my best work. I figured out how to push against it to build creative muscle and how to use its friction to spark the fire in my belly. When resistance presented an obstacle, I looked for ways over, around, or under it, finding that this approach did what an obstacle course is meant to do: it made me stronger, more resourceful, and more agile as a writer.

I started looking at each form of resistance with curiosity and a desire to understand what it could do for my writing. I studied my inner critic and its tendencies and habits, rather than trying (and failing) to ignore it, and I began to find side entrances and back doors through which I could slip to evade it. I began to use its hostile fussiness against it, antagonizing it with unruly, provocative writing until it overheated and popped.

Eventually, I gathered up all my resistance-tapping hacks and developed them into a kind of program to share with other writers. *Part Wild* is that program plus everything else I've continued to learn about resistance until this book went to press.

So here's the thing: Resistance is not futile. And it's not the enemy. In fact, it's *an asset*. This book aims to release you from a state of conflict with resistance and provide practical and fun ways to use its power in service of your creativity.

The pushback against your drive to create might be daunting, but it needn't stop you. This book reintroduces you to both sides of your creative nature in a safe and productive way. When "Get over it!" and "Just do it!" don't work, and you're just not the put-up-your-dukes type, here is another way. Eventually, the wild part of you and the tame part of you will learn each other's steps well enough to tango like a championship ballroom-dancing team.

How to Use This Book

I've intentionally made *Part Wild* accessible at any point. There is simply no wrong way to read this book: you can begin on page one and read it straight through, or you can read it back to front, or you can cherry-pick and start with the flavor of resistance that you would most like to transform from a block to a booster. Where you delve in doesn't matter.

What does matter is how you approach the prompts: your work will not be critiqued or graded, because there is no way of doing the exercises "wrong." That's the good news. The even better news? There's no way to do them right! Just as there's no "right" way to dance around your living room or play in a creek. So I encourage you to go for it and get it really wrong! Call out your wild creativity and give it permission to howl, to chase its tail, to bark down blind alleys and up wrong trees.

It's important to note that this book won't guide you in the structuring, analyzing, or editing of your work. Rather, these pages are full of cork poppers, battering rams, skeleton keys, and solvents—anything you might need to unstick or unjam your process and power up your creativity.

For best results when doing the exercises:

1. **Use pen and paper.** Even if you can type way faster than you can write, I still encourage you to use pen and paper. There is something that happens with the physical contact between the heel of your hand and the surface of the paper, the whole-arm act of moving the pen and the visceral manifesting of words in ink—a mind-body connection and sensory component that you just can't get with a keyboard.
2. **Keep your pen moving as fast as it will go.** Think of your pen as a train and your self-critical thoughts as hobos trying to hop a ride. If you write fast enough, they won't be able to jump on board.
3. **Don't think. Don't plan.** You may have the urge to think up something good before setting the timer, but if you can *think* it up, then it's something you already know. I want you to move your pen almost faster than you can think, so that you stumble onto the surprising thing that you could never get to by grinding your brain's gears. So no thinking. No planning. Just plunge.
4. **Let go of grammar, spelling, punctuation, and making sense.** Spell creatively and invent new words, flout the rules, crash the margins, mix metaphors, abuse commas, and contradict yourself. There's no red pen coming after you.
5. **Don't stop to cross anything out or correct anything.** Don't be your own red pen. There are no mistakes here—only opportunities. Just let goofs stand and keep moving forward.
6. **Don't try to be interesting, funny, or brilliant.** You want to polish and sculpt, I know. But not right now.
7. **Lose control.** When moving your pen at top speed, you might get that queasy feeling that you're about to write something terrible,

boring, gossipy, perverted, self-indulgent, whiny, trite, purple—whatever. The queasy feeling is resistance. It's telling you where the goods are. Lean in and write faster.

8. **Read it over.** Read what you've written aloud. Whether you're doing the exercises in a group or with a partner or on your own, you must read it aloud. To speed-write and leave it behind is a waste of time and effort, and reading silently to yourself will not allow you to hear what's really there. Speed-writing is a mining tool, and reading aloud is how you notice that glint of something that might lead to a vein of gold.
9. **Practice listening.** Reading aloud is an opportunity to practice *listening*—the most important skill you can develop. Drop down out of your critical mind that compares and categorizes, likes or dislikes. Listen instead with your body, your emotions, your senses, your curiosity, and your humanity. As you listen, notice your responses—a chill, stress, warmth, surprise—and whenever you respond to something, negatively or positively, underline it. Underlining doesn't mean that it meets some standard or that you have to develop it, though that's always an option. It's just another way of refining your listening practice. Identifying writing that stirs something in your senses or your gut is more useful than deciding whether you think it's any good.

About the timer: Many of the exercises are in the six-minute range. This is a carryover from the days when I was doing the timed exercises in books by teachers such as Natalie Goldberg and Deena Metzger and most of them were six minutes long. I've since come to understand that there's a good reason for this.

While on dinner break for a workshop I was teaching, I was introduced to Eleanor Criswell, who was teaching a somatic yoga course at the same institution. Eleanor studies neurophysiology, the brain-body connection, and she said that the body clenches a bit in response to any kind of change. Any time you go from one activity to another (as in, "It's time to stop looking at Twitter and write") your muscles retract—you know, just in case the new activity involves getting killed.

It makes sense that writing causes a bigger clench than some other activities. Writing invokes our fear of the dark: *What's lurking in there, beyond the light, beyond my known world? Is it a tiger, and will it chomp on my guts?* That's the question our nervous system is asking when we sit down to write.

The fight-or-flight reaction may not be noticeable to the person experiencing it, Eleanor said, but it's there. With the right equipment, it can be measured. Then she blew my mind: "And if you wait about five minutes"—Eleanor smiled—"the body calms down and unclenches all on its own."

Holy cow, I thought, *this is why the six-minute timed writing exercise works!* It's how we're wired; we just need those few minutes to relax and become available to the process. Once the timer goes off, your body will be pretty sure that if a tiger hasn't eaten you yet, it probably isn't going to. "Sure," says your body, "this activity seems to be tiger free. Go ahead and keep writing."

It can take a long time to get over one's fear of the dark, but every time you make an effort, it will pay off. The benefit is cumulative: the more times you don't get dragged under the bed by demon claws, the less frightened you will be to put your feet on the floor and make the trip to the bathroom. And the more times you sit down to write and don't go insane, or forget you have a family and responsibilities, or get swallowed whole by the great Unknown, the easier it will be to sit down to write again and again and again—six minutes at a time.

About the body map: In parts two and three of *Part Wild*, some of the prompts will make use of a "body map." In these instances, an outline of a human body will be provided, and you are invited to do the work directly in the pages of this book. You can also go to the website www.partwild.com to download and print a larger version.

About sharing: I strongly recommend that you do not read your raw exercises to anyone who's not engaged in this process. It's possible they won't have any idea how to respond and may react with awkward confusion, which is not uncommon in loved ones who celebrate our creativity but don't know how best to support it. It's not that they don't believe in us. It's just that these exercises are working the early part of the process, but when they're read aloud, they may be perceived as a finished product that needs feedback and fixing. This is like presenting your two-year-old as a PhD candidate; just because she's walking and talking and showing signs of precocious talent doesn't mean she's ready to be judged and shaped by a panel of experts. Resist the perfectly natural urge to "show them what you've been working on."

The purpose of this work is to coax your creativity out from where it's been hiding, like a cat in the rafters of the garage. I want you to reconnect with the playful and sometimes fierce part of you, the part that can make you forget to feel the passage of time or worry about what you look like. When you first let your wild thing off the leash, it might tear around the living room, overturning tables and knocking pictures off the walls, and that can be a bit intimidating. Resist the urge to shove it back into its crate. Protect it from anything that might make it shy. Give it some time and focused attention and some treats and it will eventually become your most loyal companion.

It's okay if you're nervous and light-headed. It's also okay if you're secretly excited. Who knows what really cool things might happen if you sally forth with curiosity and a sense of adventure?

Important: If at any time in your reading you are possessed by an urge to write or create, please drop this book like a hot rock and go make something!

I

Resistance Training

Building Strength and Flexibility

Why do writing exercises, you might ask? Why write *anything* that isn't going to be *something*? You should exercise your writing for the same reason you exercise your body. Walking, cycling, weight lifting, and yoga all employ the same natural force to make you strong and flexible: *resistance*. You can't build muscle without something to push against. The same goes for writing.

1

Inspiration—Fickle Muse

Don't Hold Your Breath / Provision Your Process

Until I was six years old, I loved being in water. In the desert town where I grew up, 110 degrees was the temperature on a typical summer day. Liza, the dentist's kid, had a pool, and so her house was mobbed, sunup to sundown, from when school got out in June well into October. We played Marco Polo, pretended to be mermaids, did midair contortions off the diving board, and stayed in the water until our fingers were white and wrinkled. When we got out, we'd eat sliced oranges. This was my idea of the good life.

Then my mother enrolled me in the Pollywog swimming class at the local rec center, where I was surprised to learn that I didn't know how to swim.

Every week, I suited up in my orange terry-cloth one-piece and my mom's too-big rubber swim cap with the flowers and the chin strap and marched across the nubby concrete looking like something out of Cirque du Soleil.

"Tread for five!" The college-aged instructor blew her whistle. She and all the other kids bobbed like corks while I sputtered and thrashed for the side of the pool. I just couldn't keep my head above the water. It was like trying to keep a piece of rebar afloat.

"Relaaaax." The instructor pried my fingers off the pool gutter. "Relax and feel the water pushing you to the surface." I stopped thrashing, sank, and took in water; so much for relaxing. I clawed for her shoulders and clung to them. Finally she just wore me around like a cape as she taught the other kids.

To graduate from Pollywogs, we had to swim across the short and shallow side of the pool. I splashed along like a waterwheel off its axle. When I reached the other side, purple and panting, a man with a clipboard stared at me over his glasses, puzzled. "Did you hold your breath the whole way?"

I knew I was supposed to breathe and blow bubbles, but if I lifted my head enough to get air, my bottom half sank and took the rest of me down with it. I nodded my head in shame. He marked his clipboard.

After that, I *hated* the water.

Why couldn't I float? Why couldn't I do this normal human thing? Friends tried to teach me but then watched, fascinated, as I went under. I was told I couldn't float because I was too tense, that I didn't have enough body fat, that my breathing was too shallow, my bones too dense, my muscles too stringy. I was told, and I sort of believed, that the water could sense my fear.

When I was pushing thirty, my ex-fiancé and I decided we'd like to be absolutely certain we weren't right for each other, so he took me on a vacation to the Caribbean. I was very, very nervous about snorkeling, but Greg was a champion swimmer and promised not to let me drown. In a worst-case scenario, I reasoned, I could do the cape thing and he could wear me from reef to reef.

All geared up in our snorkels, masks, and fins, we clump-slapped into the warm—wow, *waaaaarm*—water and I put my face under and I could see for miles and I pushed off and waited for the struggle and the sinking, but instead I was gliding like a water bug, flying over a bustling, colorful landscape. It was the breathing! It had always been the breathing. With the snorkel piping air down to me, I didn't have to lift my head and could lie flat as a leaf on the surface. I felt at home in the water, like it had always been my element. So *this* was floating.

There was a fleeting moment of panic when a small swell rolled over me and filled the snorkel with water, but I kept my wits and cleared the water with a big exhalation as I'd been instructed to do. Greg saw this and gave me an underwater thumbs-up. I smiled back at him around my mouthpiece.

At nearly thirty years old, I finally figured out the secret to floating, and it wasn't my attitude or my build or my worthiness. The secret was so simple I could hardly believe it. The secret was a snorkel.

Practice #1: Don't Hold Your Breath

I adored swimming until I "learned to swim." This is a perfect corollary for the experience of all the writers who've told me, "Writing used to be effortless and fun, but now it's a struggle. It's heartbreak. It's fraught. It's torture." That charged intensity that once made you want to spend every minute writing isn't necessarily permanent. It's the tugboat that pulled you out to sea, effortless and dreamy, but at some point, you need to continue of your own volition. When the mild insanity of infatuation dissipates, it doesn't mean the relationship is over. Well, okay, with Greg and me it did, but couples who stay together must find new ways to kindle their connection. It's the same with creative inspiration.

When I first started writing, I thought that if I was truly inspired, I should be able to just dive into my chair and float along on a warm, welcoming current of words. I'd sit there, pen poised, a willing vessel, waiting for the muse to love me up and send something through.

Waiting for inspiration is like holding your breath.

After a lot of frustrated waiting, I thought, *What the heck is inspiration, anyway?* I realized I had no idea. I thought back to how our voice teacher in acting school used to chant, "Iiiiin-spire . . . Eeeex-pire . . ." to cue our breaths in and out. According to etymonline.com, "inspire" originally meant "to breathe in," or, more literally, "to inhale spirit." *All right*, I thought, *if I'd waited to grow gills, I'd never have gotten to see a coral reef. If I want to swim in deep inspirational waters, I'll need the creative equivalent of a snorkel and fins.*

I'm not saying that your process can't revolve around a Muse or a Source or a Higher Power, but the problem with outsourcing inspiration is that it can prevent the formation of method. You can keep yourself afloat and propel your pen into new and unexpected waters. You absolutely can. You just need to provision your process with the proper gear and develop your method.

Everyone's process is unique, so the gear and the method will vary widely. Where I need a snorkel, you might do better with a pool noodle. Then again, you might need a full-on boat with an outboard motor. The first step is to get intimate with your process and notice what it needs.

Prompt: The Process of Noticing Your Process

One of your most powerful creative tools is Noticing with a capital N. Before you can provision yourself for a creative outing, you must first understand the physics of your creative element and the assumptions you have about it. Here are a few ways to start tracking these things, but know that the process of noticing your process should be ongoing.

Step One: Start a list entitled "Iiiiiin-spire" and jot down anything you can think of that "oxygenates" your creativity and makes you want to write or make art. For instance: *loud symphonic music*; *a walk in nature*; *prayer (or meditation)*; *reading my favorite poet*; *uncouth, foolish dancing*. List for six minutes. Keep the list handy, and any time you notice something else that floats your creative boat, add it to the list.
Step Two: Start a list entitled "Eeeeeex-pire" and fill it with creative sinkers. This list is for anything that deflates your creative spirit. For instance: *fatigue or hunger*; *the incessant barking of the dog next door*; *a sore back*; *money worries*; *a lack of ideas.* List for six minutes. Continue to list sinkers as you notice them.
Step Three: Start a list entitled "Everything I Know about Inspiration" and fill it with any beliefs, superstitions, or ideas—helpful or unhelpful—you have about where creativity comes from. For instance: *I have to be inspired to write*; *only real geniuses get inspired*; *if the writing feels "tight" it won't be any good*; *if I am pleasing to the muse, she will favor me with brilliance.* List for six minutes.
Step Four: Examine these beliefs and decide 1) whether they're true, and 2) whether they support your creativity. Any time you discover another unexamined assumption about inspiration, add it to the list.

Practice #2: Provision Your Process

As soon as I stopped looking for inspiration, I was able to see what was right in front of me—my own process. For instance, I used to think that drowsiness was a sign of weakness until I remembered it was actually a sign of tiredness, and I didn't write well when I was tired. I dragged a small sofa into my writing room and placed it right next to my desk so I could tumble out of my chair onto a comfy surface to give my brain a break. I would wake from these power naps fresh and ready for action, and often I'd have a little dream or a half-conscious waking thought to propel me back to my writing with something new.

My write-and-nap method was validated when I toured George Bernard Shaw's home and saw that his teeny writing cabin featured a slim sleeping platform directly behind his chair so that he could tip right over for a lie-down.

It's also noteworthy that the cabin sat on a device that allowed him to turn the whole structure and follow or escape the direct sunlight throughout the day. Here's a writer who studied his process, figured out what best supported it, and built it to spec.

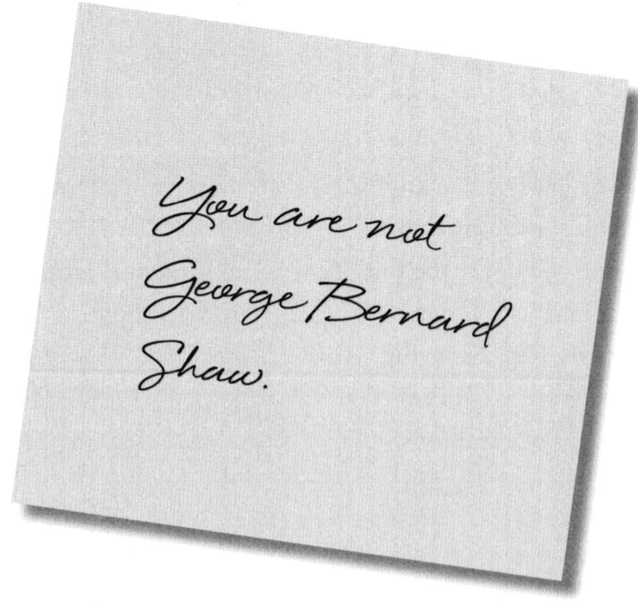
You are not
George Bernard
Shaw.

By this I mean that your process is your own, unique and incomparable. What worked for Shaw or Shakespeare or Sidney Sheldon may not work for you. I used to devour author interviews and writers' memoirs searching for the magic bullet. I especially wanted to lift from the authors I truly admired: what were the habits, traits, and tendencies that allowed them to be so prolific, or so profound?

They said things like, "I sit down to write and don't get up until I reach my page goal, no matter what."

"I get up every forty-five minutes and do a non-writing activity, no matter what."

"Writing must be treated like a job."

"Writing must feel like play."

"A writing space separate from the house is essential."

"I can't write anywhere but at the kitchen counter."

"There must be a window with a view."

"If there's a window, I can't write."

"There has to be music."

"I must have total silence."

I wanted to take their secrets as gospel, but unfortunately successful authors have conflicting secrets, because every author is different.

Here's a short list of provisions I came up with after a careful study of my own process needs:

* A warm beverage in an insulated cup—If my tea stays hot, it's easier to stay in my chair.
* Prompts—They're the fins of my writing process, propelling me along until I see something I can get curious about.
* A timer—It's like having a personal coach that I have to obey.
* Chewing gum—It deflects most resistance-driven snack attacks.
* Back stretches and twists—They keep me from being pushed out of my chair by pain.

* A space heater, a blanket, and warm socks—Being cold is just upsetting.
* A window that opens onto a view—This keeps me from feeling imprisoned.
* A snoring dog nearby—It's like a meditation, a mantra, and sanctification all rolled into one.
* A writer-friendly café—This gets me away from the dusting and dishes that nag.
* Headphones—At the café, listening to music without lyrics provides insulation from nearby conversations and the buzz of blenders without interrupting the flow of words. At home, headphones signal to my husband not to speak to me.
* A separate drop-down desk for bill paying, budgeting, and to-do ticking—This keeps practical worries out of my line of sight when I write. Just close the lid on that nonsense.
* Lip balm—I try never to write without it, which means buying quite a few and having them all around. It also means I have to check my pockets extra carefully on laundry day or risk coconut-oil spots all over my favorite skirt. However, if you think about it, what's more distracting than chapped lips when you're trying to concentrate?

So don't go and build a rotating cabin because it worked for Shaw. The page you want to take from his book is that he found out what made his writing go and he gave himself that.

Prompt: Take Stock

Step One: Make a careful and detailed list of what is and isn't working in your writing environment. Think about your five senses and how they're being soothed or aggravated. Is it bright enough? What's in your line of vision? Is your chair comfortable? How's the temperature? Keep this environmental inventory at hand.

Step Two: Read over your environmental inventory and choose something that really poses a problem. Write that thing at the top of the next blank space—for example, *The neighbor works on his motorcycle and revs the engine repeatedly for hours.*

Good. Now, underneath that, write the reasons this poses a problem—for example, *I can't think about what I want to write because all I can think about is how outrageously rude my neighbor is.*

Step Three: Brainstorm ways to work with this issue. Don't stop to "think up something really good." Put down everything from the obvious to the ridiculous to the illegal. For instance: *talk to my neighbor*; *shoot my neighbor dead*; *get noise-canceling headphones and replace revving with rainforest sounds*; *shoot my neighbor's motorcycle.* List for six minutes.

Some issues can be solved without brainstorming—once the problem is identified, the solution becomes obvious. If the sun blasts your desk, get a window shade. If you get hungry, install a fruit bowl in your study, or maybe an electric kettle and a collection of instant soups. Other issues, such as self-doubt and distraction, may take some time to solve, or even to recognize. That's all right. Just commit to a conscious and proactive relationship with your process and read on.

Bonus Prompts: An Array of Process Buoys to Explore

While it's true that one artist's secrets may not be transferable to another, it is possible that the process fix you're looking for has already been discovered by someone else. After all, I didn't invent the snorkel. Here are some novel work-arounds that I've come across in my work with writers:

Stay in your pajamas and don't fix your hair. If you're not fit to be seen, you're less likely to give in to the urge to run to the store or the post office or to do whatever it is that seems so much more urgent than writing.

Get an app that disables social media, but not the Internet. You want to keep yourself from wasting time cruising Facebook and Pinterest, but still be able to use online dictionary and etymology sites. Think of it like a snorkel—it gives you breathing room.

Lock the study/bedroom/garage/bathroom door. There's no law against locking the door. Put up one of those little plastic clock signs that lets your family know when you'll be back. They'll be okay without you for a few hours at a stretch.

Hire the teen next door to play a board game with your kids for a few hours. It's just a few bucks, and if you spend the time writing, you get a big return on your investment.

Do writing prompts with your kids. If you can't get time off from the kids, enlist them. Most kids (as well as spouses, friends, and elderly live-in parents) really enjoy doing writing or drawing prompts. It'll buy you five to fifteen minutes of writing at a stretch and can only bring you closer to your loved ones and get them excited about this writing thing of yours.

Write in thirty- to forty-five-minute intervals with ten-minute breaks for dancing, playing with the cat, or folding laundry. While writing in timed intervals can feel like cheating or goofing off, it's really a great way to set yourself up for success. Knowing you have a little break coming up can make it easier to sit still. Plus, our best creative thinking happens when we aren't "thinking." If you step away from the computer and give your mind a chance to slip into that drifting mode where it can make random associations without the pressure to produce results, you are likely to have story problems solved for you and discoveries delivered unbidden. This method has the added benefit of letting the restless part of you think it's getting away with something.

Take your fingers off the keyboard and use pen and paper. Most of us don't even notice that we've been staring at a blinking cursor for ten minutes. We don't register our stalled state until we see that we've picked all the nail polish off our fingernails. While some writers are freed up by the speed of the keyboard, lots of folks are instead drawn into a thinking/editing mode—something about that Delete key being *right there*. The feeling of pen on paper is more physical, more muscular. The sensation of releasing ink onto paper is visceral and coaxes us down from the brain and into the body, where we can explore with our emotions and senses rather than planning and choosing and judging with our thinking mind.

Use a timer. If you don't have someone telling you, "Just half a page more and you're done! You can do it, I know you can!" a timer can be the next best thing when it comes to keeping your pen moving.

Use an hourglass. For the steampunk writers among you.

Use a junk book. It's pretty annoying when I'm writing at a good clip and an unrelated idea jumps into my head. It might be an idea for another story, or a solution to a marital disagreement, or a realization that I forgot to change my address with the DMV. I don't want to lose the idea, but I don't want to stop writing, so I keep a junk book nearby expressly for the purpose of catching any thoughts that are not pertinent to the work at hand. Later, I'll go through today's "junk" and input it into my to-do list, calendar, or good-ideas file.

Get a room. Or don't. Taking Virginia Woolf's words to heart, many writers will make it their mission to create the perfect writing room; I did. First I moved into the spare room. Then I decided I needed a space separate from the house and bought a vintage camping trailer. Cleaning that thing took two weeks, and my husband had to custom-build a desk for it. In the end, it was fabulous—the best writing cave ever. Unfortunately, I never wrote in there. I found I did my best writing at the dining room table, or on the sofa with the dogs, or at the café with my earbuds in. A writing room works for many people, but if it's not for you, let it go. You might like to write standing up in the laundry room with the dryer running. You might like to write under a tree. Find your power spot.

Rent a cheap hotel room in a town you don't care to visit. Several times during our many years together, I've asked my husband to send me away for my birthday to do some deeper work on a project. My favorite place is Desert Hot Springs, California, because the hotels are super cheap and all have hot mineral pools, and the town, with its high winds and lack of natural beauty, is almost hostile to exploration, making confinement very doable. Isolation isn't everyone's cup of tea, but if you can swing it, it can be wonderful for the easily distracted introvert, especially when starting or finishing a draft.

Write on napkins, Post-its, and receipts. If you're just scribbling on a scrap of paper—why not a toilet-paper roll or a coffee cup?—your inner perfectionist probably won't even wake up.

Ritualize and reward. My friend Gordon burns his notes nightly in a wheelbarrow in the backyard as a reward for having addressed them all. If he does his work, he gets to satisfy his inner pyromaniac.

Think in deadlines or tiny bites. Some writers would never finish a project without a deadline. For others, deadlines are the headlights to their deer. Deadline-positive writers, get yourself some accountability—court a publishing deal, join a writing group, line up contest submission dates on your calendar. Deadline-averse writers, detach from the long-term goal and break things into tiny bites—commit to two paragraphs a day, write in timed six-minute bursts, make your commitment infinitely *doable*. You can get a lot of words on the page in just six minutes.

Keep yourself in finger puppets, bendy toys, Play-Doh, Sculpey, or crayons and large lengths of butcher paper. What do you do when your mind's gears start grinding? On my desk, I have a finger-puppet monster perched on a bottle. He's red and yellow and his skinny rubber arms are open wide, like he wants to run at me for a hug, like he hopes to be tickled, like he wants to give me the old razzmatazz. He says, "Draw the feeling that you're trying to describe. What color is it? Grab a crayon!" He points frantically to the hunk of modeling clay and urges me to "just think about the story and make a shape." He says, "Get me off this bottle and let's improv the scene!" He really is a ham. Sometimes we need a monster to remind us that there are lots of ways to get over ourselves and get it in gear.

2

Imagination-Shy Mind

Give Your Thoughts Some Privacy/ Induce Daydreaming

To keep myself in cheese sandwiches during acting school, I babysat for the teachers and the actors in the company. I wasn't a great babysitter—I'm a nervous person, and kids are very unpredictable. But while my childcare wasn't inspired, I could make "kid food" and see to it that no one was badly injured.

One of my charges was Avery, a smart, rosy two-year-old. I couldn't get Avery to say my name. She could say lots of words and was already stringing sentences together, so I took it personally. Bending down, hands on knees, I coaxed, "Say 'Deb.' Come on, Aves, say 'Deeeeeeeb,'" and she would get really interested in stacking her blocks.

I was arranging some cut-up weenies—this was before food was local or organic—in a happy face on a plate when I heard her singsongy little voice behind me. She was facing into a corner behind a kitchen chair, whisper-practicing my name: "De-buh, De-buh, Deb."

Poor kid. I was giving her stage fright. All she needed was a little privacy.

Practice #3: Give Your Thoughts Some Privacy

When you go over to a new friend's house for dinner, you enter through the front door and are greeted by your friend and her husband, who merrily bring you into their spacious kitchen and chat with you while seamlessly sharing the dinner prep. They're clearly progressive thinkers, equals who still find each other irresistible. The house is clean and ready for its close-up, and the kids are bright and polite with just the right amount of quirk.

But come back tomorrow at dinnertime and spy on them through the window. No, I don't really want you to spy on your friend, silly. But if you did, you'd see an entirely different family. One child sits two inches from the TV while their overweight Chihuahua eats from the ignored bowl of mac and cheese in her lap. The so-called quiet one is doing a slanderous impression of his gym teacher. Your friend searches under the furniture, dust bunnies in her hair, trying to find the hamster before the cat does, screeching at her husband to help while he ignores her in favor of playing Angry Birds.

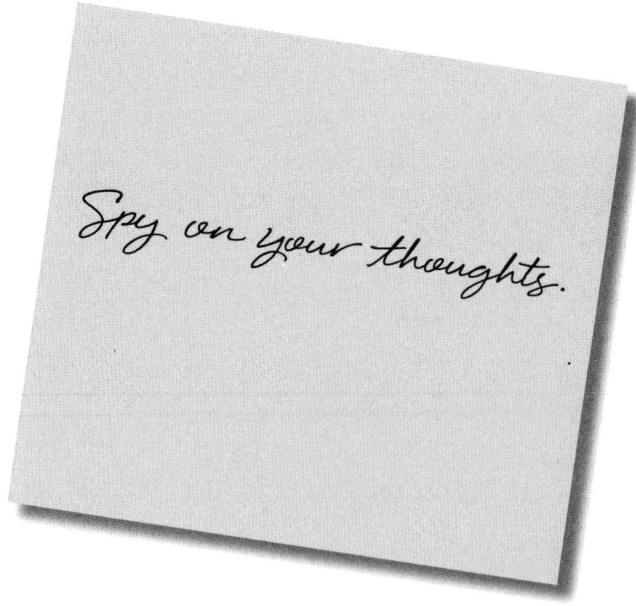

Thinking is your brain's version of hard staring, and memory and meaning are shy. When you confront them straight on and demand that they deliver, they try too hard to impress you, and things get awkward. Thinking and trying harder don't work any better for generating fresh ideas than they do for improving your dancing or making you hotter in bed. However, if you coax your mind into a sense of privacy, your ideas, memories, and sparks of genius can loosen up and get real.

Prompt: Loosen Up Your Thoughts with a List

Lists are wonderful because your mind doesn't see them as writing. "Oh, you're only making a list?" your mind says. "Well, let me know when you do some real writing."

Make a list of all the vehicles you've ever been in. Cars, trucks, motorcycles, barges—anything with an engine and a driver goes on this list. Go for quantity. Don't describe. Just list. Write for six minutes. Save the list for use in Practice #4.

Bonus Prompts: More Uses for Listing and Spying

- If you have to write a love scene and you feel stuck or self-conscious, you might try a list of all the kisses you've given or received or all the types of kisses you can think of.
- If you're writing about your family, try making a list of all the bathing suits you've ever worn to scare up some vacations or outings.
- Shoes you've owned or worn, doors you've opened, and trees you've known are all good launch points for lists.
- Make a list of all the bedrooms you've ever been in. Bathrooms are also great, because that's where we do a lot of our locked-door stuff.

Any of the above lists is good for discovering juicy or revealing details about your characters. What kisses do they remember? What cars have they ridden in? What trees have they climbed, sat under, played around, swung from? What foods can't they eat? What smells would they take to heaven?

Feel free to spy on one of your characters through a window while he goes about his business. Watch him get ready for a date; watch his bathroom rituals. Go through his glove compartment and look under his car seat. Look under the bed. See if he has anything hidden at the back of his closet. Go through his pockets. What does he do when he's finally alone in the house? How does he behave behind the wheel? Take notes like a private detective who knows how to use a telephoto lens, pick a lock, and bug a phone.

Practice #4: Induce Daydreaming

When you're engaged in the serious business of life, your mind helps you out by eliminating distracting thoughts so you can focus on the task at hand. For obvious reasons, this is a very good thing when you're doing something like driving in traffic, where your focus is the key to your safety. But if your mind is white-knuckling it when you focus, for instance, on a question like "What's interesting about this character?" it will freeze out 99 percent of your thoughts, dismissing them as trivial, too weird, or not good enough. This may keep you from getting into a wreck, but it's not going to help you with creating your story.

In creative matters, we want to be less like the focused driver and more like children in the backseat, engrossed in a play battle in which the car seats are dragon saddles and the sippy cups are sword handles. Children at play are immersed, focused, and full of serious intent. But if you ask them what they're doing, they won't say, "I'm performing a dragon battle." Rather, they say, "I'm just playing," or "I'm just pretending."

The mental equivalent of playing is daydreaming—that relaxed-but-intent state in which the mind loses its performance anxiety. This is the dance-like-no-one-is-watching brain state where everything gets groovy.

This is the reason you have some of your best creative ideas when you're in the shower, walking, or just waking up. Because your brain isn't engaged in "serious business," your guard goes down and the alpha waves kick up so your wilder, weirder, more surprising thoughts can go surfing.

But unlike ocean waves, you don't have to wait for this daydreaming state to arise: you can induce it. All you need is a way to tempt your mind into a state of intent playfulness.

Because who has time to wait for their thoughts to relax and feel safe? Life is short, my friend, and you have a full-time job, three kids, a needy cat, and a roof that needs fixing. When you get a half hour to write, you want to get right to the good stuff.

Prompt: Go Along for the Ride

Step One: Choose a car from the list in the previous prompt. Any car that draws your attention or makes you curious is great. If you have a hard time choosing, choose three and then eliminate two. Write the chosen car or vehicle at the top of the next blank space. For example: *primer-gray El Camino*; *Kawasaki 500*; *Dad's Charger*; *Mrs. Shelton's minivan.*

Step Two: Write everything you know about the chosen vehicle. Describe the car in as much detail as you can—color, make, model, features. Don't discriminate against the obvious bits, such as, "It has bugs on the windshield and two headlights, one of which is cracked." Then climb into the car. What was your designated seat—driver's, shotgun, backseat? Take up your position and write everything you can see, smell, feel, taste, or hear from this spot. Look out the window, under the seats, and in the glove box. Are there Cheerios on the floor and the smell of spoiled milk? Is the upholstery hot from the sun? Is there anything hanging from the rearview mirror? Are the windows open or closed? What's the air like outside? Write down all the details you can, in no particular order. Write for six minutes.

Step Three: Be a backseat driver. Figuratively let go of the wheel and go wherever the car wants to go. It might take you someplace you've been. It might take you someplace new. Don't think. Don't try to steer it someplace interesting or capture the meaning of the journey. Just be a passenger, keep your pen moving, and let the car do the work. Write for six minutes or more.

Bonus Prompts: More Lists to Play With

* Make a list entitled "Shoes I've Worn." Include formal shoes, shoes that hurt your feet, sports shoes, work shoes, casual shoes,

and indoor-only shoes. Choose a pair, put them on, and let them take you on a walk.

* Make a list of your favorite characters from fiction, movies, history, and your own work. Choose one to spend some time with. Ask this character to take you to a favorite spot or to a secret spot.
* Make a list of smells you love or hate. Choose one. Let the smell take you back to a place and time when you smelled it a lot.
* Make a list entitled "Roads Not Taken." Set out on one with the attitude of an explorer and record what you observe.

3

Distraction—Monkey Mind

Point Your Mind / Don't "Just Do It"

On the day we second graders were to take the Bicycle Road Safety Certificate test, I rode my purple-sparkle bike with the handlebar streamers to school instead of taking the bus. I loved my bike. It was almost a part of me. I was going to ace the test.

During second period, we skipped spelling and walked our bikes out to the blacktop of the schoolyard, where the local policemen had set up an obstacle course of orange pylons and flags. There was a little bridge thing in the middle—maybe I would stand on my pedals going over that, just kinda casual. That would be cool. I nosed my front wheel up to the starting line, and when the officer blew his whistle, I launched.

I made it through the first part okay, though I felt a little shaky. As I approached the bridge, my nerves jumped. It was impossibly narrow, the edges shrinking toward each other as I crossed it. I panic-braked, wobbled off the edge, and flailed into a heap.

The officer charged with my bicycle safety education told me, "Go ahead and give it another shot."

Walking my bike to the back of the line, I hated my handlebar streamers. They were stupid. *Why did my parents get me a bike with streamers?*

I blew it two more times. My bike felt like something unnatural beneath me. I strangled the handgrips, and my front wheel jerked like a live thing toward the pylons. I should have practiced more. It was like I was magnetized to the pylons and to the edges of that stupid, stupid bridge. Maybe I wasn't as good a rider as I thought. I could feel my chin quivering. *No, no, no. Don't cry! You're such a dork. You might as well just pee your pants right here in front of everybody.*

The officer studied me, pulling on his mustache. "Looks like you're running into some trouble there, my friend."

"I'm trying not to hit all that stuff, but—" *Don't cry!*

"Hmmmm. How about you go back to the starting line, and this time, don't look where you *don't* want to go."

"Well, then where do I—oh."

I glued my eyes to the space in front of my tire, only seeing the next few inches of blacktop, which I chomp-chomp-chomped with each pump of the pedals. The pylons and flags disappeared. I sailed over the bridge and flew around the kickball circle without even wobbling, and then rode under the banner that said "Finish Line!" The officer grinned. "Nice work, kiddo!" He patted me kind of too hard on the back and handed me my road-ready certificate.

Practice #5: Point Your Mind

You read somewhere that you should treat writing like a job, so promptly at 9:00 a.m. you sit down to write. Immediately, you're restless. You bite your pen. You stare out the window at the weeds growing in your garden. It wouldn't take long to pull them, and the fresh air might do you good. No, stop it. Eyes on the screen. Focus. You open your e-mail. Maybe you'll be able to concentrate better if you just fire off a response to that passive-aggressive message from your mother-in-law, clear some headspace. You castigate yourself for your lack of discipline and *will* yourself to focus. Pen biting. Window gazing. Weeds. E-mail. The chair becomes more and more uncomfortable until it ejects you like a piece of toast and you find yourself weeding instead of writing.

Life is always happening—even when we're trying to get quiet and write—so we need to learn to manage our attention. To do this, we need to understand how attention works.

When I was trying to ride my bike through the training course, the obstacles loomed large, to the point where I could think of nothing but their potential to defeat or hurt me, what they meant about my lack of skill, and how I wanted to prove them wrong. However, when I gave my mind something of equal or greater appeal to focus on, the obstacles ceased to have power over me.

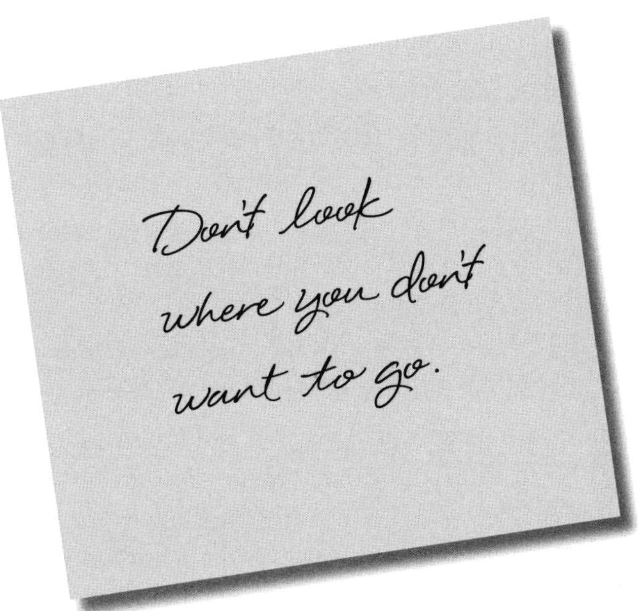
Don't look
where you don't
want to go.

There are the real difficulties that life hands us, and then there are the hot little dramas that we fuel with our preoccupation. We all have our own inner drama queen, the part of us that likes to pour gas on the fire and get pulled into the adrenaline rush the combustion causes. But this always takes us in the opposite direction of our writing. If you have a lot of drama in your life, and it keeps you from your work, first, notice it. Because if you don't identify it, it can work on you unconsciously. Then decide whether your attention will suppress or inflame the drama. For instance, a smarty-pants reply to your mother-in-law's e-mail will undoubtedly kindle the conflict. It's a clear case of "you can be right or you can write." So put that in the "drama" column.

Next, withdraw your attention from the drama. This will have the same effect as withdrawing oxygen from a fire. You don't even have to put the fire out. You just have to quit feeding it.

As my wise hippie friends like to remind me, "Energy flows where attention goes." The big question is how do you point your mind at getting the book done when it still craves a win with your mother-in-law, damn her.

The long-term goal of "getting the book done" isn't something your mind can get its teeth into. It's so far in the future, and who even knows what's involved in getting there? The weeds are right here, right now. Pull 'em. Done. And pressing Send on an e-mail—so immediate, so satisfying.

When all the mind has to go on is how far off the goal is and how strenuous it will be to get there, it will lobby for procrastination, but tempt it with incremental successes and it's back on board. I remember hearing Oprah talk about training for a marathon and how much she hated running up hills until her coach told her, "Watch your feet." When she took her eyes off the far-off crest that would bring relief and glued them to her sneakers, she could trick her mind into believing there was no hill at all—just road, and she was putting that behind her.

In order to get through the obstacle course, I didn't focus on the finish line. I focused on the blacktop in front of my tire. It was all kinds of satisfying to pull that little patch of tar under my wheel. The writing version of this perspective is prompts. Prompts lure your mind away from the long-term goal and the obstacles that await by giving it a more immediate and engaging task.

Prompt: Everything I Know About . . .

The "Everything I Know About . . ." prompt is very flexible. It can be used to excavate, pry open, or perk up just about any topic. Most often, you know more than your mind would have you think. This is a good tool to use when you think you don't know anything, think there's nothing new or interesting to know, or think what there is to know is too big.

In this instance, we're going to use it to point your mind at something immediate in order to draw it away from all the worries on the sidelines.

Step One: "Everything I Know About My Body Right Now." Describe everything you know about your current physical state of being: the temperature inside and outside your body, how your hair feels on your head, what your mouth tastes like, your aches and pains. Any time your mind wants to wander, get interested again in what's happening in your body. Don't try to be lyrical or original. Notice any desire to be interesting, funny, or even coherent and flick it away. Just inventory. Write for six minutes.

Step Two: "Everything I Know About My Project Right Now." Write everything you currently know about your story, documentary, painting, or whatever it is you're working on. Write about characters, images, themes. Whatever is top-of-mind, put it down on paper. If you keep getting an image of a woman with a melon-green purse, write that. If it takes place in another solar system, or someone will be poisoned, or a paisley print couch is prominently featured, write that. Just move your pen as fast as it will go and fill the page with no regard to order or sense. Write for six minutes.

Step Three: Go back over this writing and underline anything that has a little energy to it. Grab one of those underlined items and use it to launch your pen on another six-minute dash. Rather than overwhelming your mind with the work yet to be done, this prompt points your mind at the aspects of your project that are currently of interest and have the power to draw you in.

Practice #6: Don't "Just Do It"

I tried for years to discipline myself to "just do it." I tried writing in the same place at the same time every day. I yelled at myself. I rewarded myself. I wrote a large check to the Westboro Baptist Church and told my husband to mail it if I didn't meet my page quota. I meditated. I sequestered myself in the woods, in the desert, in a garret, in Hawaii. Discipline didn't bloom in me. It was a mortifying cycle; the more I tightened down on the discipline, the less I wrote.

It's one of the great puzzles of the writing life: if writing is what you live for, how come you're so easily seduced away from it by a weedy garden? It makes sense, if you think about it. Writing, while it's clearly one of the most enriching things we do, can take us to some pretty challenging places. Putting aside the hell-and-back emotional rides you go on with your characters, there is also the great un-knowing of it all. You don't know where the writing is going, when or if you'll be finished, or what dark corner of your own psyche it might draw you into. Who wouldn't take weeds over that? You know when you start weeding pretty much how it's going to go and that you will be rewarded for your hard work with freshly revealed flowers.

But you still have to write. So what to do?

Instead of valuing the discipline, willpower, and drive that serve us in the achievement sector, writing likes us soft and vulnerable. I'm not saying that self-discipline doesn't exist. I know people who have it, and it works for them. But trying harder, self-castigation, and the marshaling of willpower will not keep most writers in the chair. In fact, the harder we work the discipline angle the more likely the weeds are to win. Neuroscience research shows that exerting willpower is highly taxing for the brain. Like running on your toes, using your willpower puts all the stress on a muscle that's not designed for long-distance work—you'll have a more successful 5K if you involve your quads, glutes, and hamstrings. In other words, the more you bear down on your willpower, the sooner you want a cookie and a nap.

So, how do we soften *and* get the writing done?

In the now famous "Marshmallow Test," kids were put in a room with a bell and two plump, snowy-white marshmallows on a plate. They were told, "I'm going to leave the room. You can ring this bell and I will come right back and you can have one treat, but if you wait until I return on my own, you can have *both*." Then they were left alone with the treats for fifteen minutes, or for as long as they could resist ringing the bell. The agony and antics that were caught on the hidden camera as these children tried to resist temptation are heartrending and hilarious.

Many, many people have used the Marshmallow Test to talk about the importance of self-discipline and "grit," because the kids who delayed gratification and held out for the second marshmallow were reportedly more successful later in life.

I've watched a great many videos of these kids, partly because they're very entertaining. More interesting to me, though, was the how of it. *How* did they resist temptation? Were some kids just naturally gifted with self-discipline?

When I watched these videos, what I saw was not self-discipline or willpower. The kids who earned that second marshmallow were not sitting there all steely, staring the marshmallow down. Rather, they were staring into the middle distance, clearly daydreaming, taking themselves far away from the object of torment, or they were busily investigating their bodies and their clothes and the room. Many explored the marshmallow itself, turning it from an object of conflict to an object of curiosity, squishing it, rolling it, smelling it, licking it, making it the subject of a song, finding all the things they could do to it besides eat it. One video had photos of the marshmallows that had made it through this phase of the test, and they were a wreck—pocked and creased and misshapen as though they had been through durability testing.

My personal and very unscientific conclusion is that the children who were successful in resisting the marshmallow didn't count on their Marine-like discipline because they didn't have any. They're just little kids. Instead, they employed their curiosity and imagination to point their minds away from temptation. One child said she imagined a frame around the treat and "pretended it was just a picture of a marshmallow."

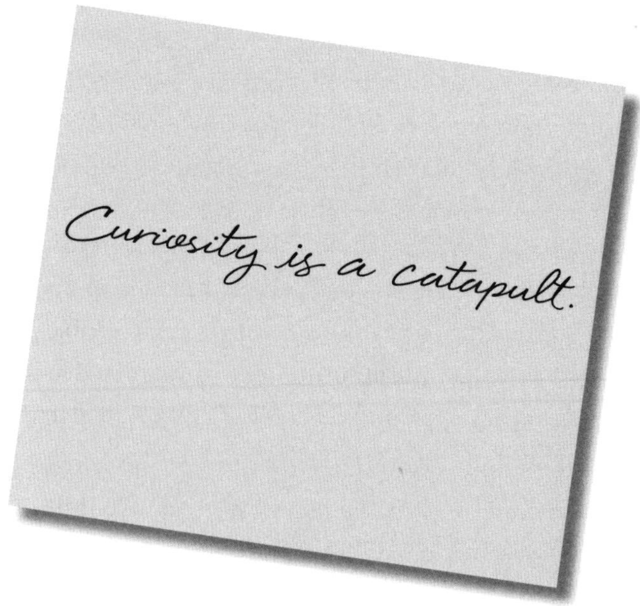
Curiosity is a catapult.

There are few forces on earth more powerful than curiosity. Curiosity has propelled many an explorer away from the safety and comforts of civilization to brave unknown and potentially hostile conditions. The need to know is so strong that it even gets them past their fear of failure and their prime directive to stay alive. If curiosity can do that for an explorer, it will surely drag you by your hair—past to-do lists and drama and earthly delights and needy spouses and worries—right into the uncharted territory of your own work. Unlike willpower, curiosity and imagination don't wear out with use. They're infinitely renewable and clean burning.

Saying you can't write if you're not disciplined is like saying you can't climb a mountain if you're not a goat. If you're not a naturally disciplined person and you're not likely to become one anytime soon, that's fine. Get curious about what's on top of the mountain, and you'll find a way to get up there.

Prompt: Get Curious

Step One: "Everything I Know About You." Choose someone that you *don't* know, someone who piques your curiosity. If you're writing in a public place, just look up and choose someone in your range of vision. If not, you might pick the lady behind the counter at the 7-Eleven where you fill up your car—someone who made an impression, but whom you know little about. Write everything you know about this person: she has the thickest hair you've ever seen and she wears several rings on each finger. She's had a terrible cough for weeks. Don't worry about capturing her character in detail, just put down everything that comes to mind in no particular order. Write for six minutes.

Step Two: "Everything I *Don't* Know About You." Working with the same subject, write all the things you don't know about her. For instance: *I don't know if she has kids or what that tattoo is that peeks out from her sleeve. I don't know what she keeps in the pockets of her smock*. Don't strive to get at something interesting. Just get curious and write whatever comes up. Write for six minutes.

Step Three: "Everything I Don't Know About My Project." Repeat step two, but apply the prompt to your project. Write everything you don't know—how it ends, what it's really about, why you're drawn to the subject matter. Is there a character that is eluding you? Instead of trying to "make her interesting," see if you can get curious about her the way you did about the 7-Eleven woman. Why does she use such big words? What is her middle name? How come she won't eat what her husband cooks? How come she always wears blue? Write for six minutes.

Step Four: Follow Your Curiosity. Read through the writing from step three and underline anything that you really would like to know more about, then use that as a launchpad. By pursuing things you wish to know more about, you can plug yourself back into the energy that launched the project in the first place. So often, our creative urges are just helping us get to the next thing we're trying to know and understand.

- If you want to know why your character bites his thumbs, try asking him, "Why do you do that?" Write down his answer.
- If you want to know where a character hides something, search his house and car, writing down everything you find.
- If you want to know how your story ends, try writing all the possible ways you think it could end. Try asking your story how it *wants* to end.
- If you want to know why hedgehogs keep showing up in your paintings, write six minutes of "Everything I Know About Hedgehogs" (but do this *before* googling hedgehogs).

Bonus Prompts: More "Everything I Know About"s

Noticing what you *don't* know is a great way to find out what you *wish* to know. Notice what makes you curious. Notice how curiosity feels in your body. Notice how you feel when your curiosity is engaged. If you understand how curiosity works, you will be better able to use it to further your creative endeavors.

Write everything you know about ice cubes for six minutes without stopping your pen; you'll find there's way more to an ice cube than you thought. Also try paper clips, end tables, box hedges, and guppies.

Write everything you know about clichéd topics, like love or sunsets or anything that's lost its freshness due to overexploration. It might take you six minutes just to get through the top layer of clichés—*love is patient*; *love is the answer*; *love is a many-splendored thing*—so be prepared to write for another six minutes to get beyond the easier answers your mind wants to hand you. Also try dark and stormy nights, spring flowers, and orphans.

Write everything you know about a topic you know nothing about. Before you do any research, speed-write everything you already know about it, allowing yourself to guess, assume, and make stuff up.

4

Perfectionism—Picking and Polishing

Blow By the Pebbles

Back in the nineties, when in-line skates were all the rage, I thought, "Eureka! This will be the perfect way to get around New York!" My friend Gillian from acting school waited tables in them, skated on and off the subway in them, and clumped up and down stairs in them. If I navigated the city on blades, I thought, I would put a crazy amount of hours back in my schedule.

In the park, in my new skates, I wobbled from tree to street sign to park bench thinking if I was careful and took it slow, I'd avoid injury, learn faster, and be on my way to being a whiz on wheels, just like Gillian. I was amazed and very, very discouraged to find that the tiniest pebble on the road could take me down. Wobble, wobble, pebble, *wham*! I was getting my money's worth out of my kneepads and wrist guards. After days of this, I was thinking I'd made a big mistake. These deathtraps had not been cheap, and I wasn't going to save any time at all if I couldn't even skate as fast as I walked. I put off calling Gillian for help because, well, let's just say she had an unacknowledged impulse control issue. Finally, though, I got frustrated enough and asked her to meet me in the park.

"You're going too slow," she said. "Faster! Go faster!"

"You're kidding, right? I can barely stay up at a crawl."

With a characteristic lack of warning, she grabbed my hand and took off, hauling me behind her like a trailer with a bum wheel.

"Bend your knees! Go, go, go! C'mon!"

She had a firm grip on me. I could either pump like an Olympic speed skater or get dragged onto my face. I pumped and swooshed, pumped and swooshed. I was swooshing. I was staying up! I was sailing over pebbles with the wind rushing by and I could feel my center of gravity like a gyroscope, connecting me to the earth.

Practice #7: Blow By the Pebbles

When you're in perfectionist mode, you sweat every pebble for its potential to take you down. You slow to a crawl, your gyroscope putzes out, and you grab for the nearest tree—and there you stay.

Perfectionism consists of endless negotiations, judgments, and comparisons, all of which seem to be life-and-death. You fuss and finesse while perfectionism spins you into a sticky web of self-consciousness so thick you can no longer hear the heartbeat of your story. One of the biggest problems with perfectionism is that it goads you into rewriting before you've even *written*.

We all know what's really at stake here. The F-word: *failure*. You put your soul into this thing and you can't stand the thought of being laughed at or misunderstood. If you strive for perfection you'll prevent failure. Right? Wrong.

There is no "perfect" in art because art is subjective. There is only striving and reaching. This is the reason for the helmet, wrist guards, and kneepads: if you're all in, falling is a given. No Olympic athlete ever made it to the games without first falling hundreds of times, because falling and failing are the result of courting the next level of skill. The masters learn the art of falling well.

So, gear up, go faster, and fall safely. Create an environment that celebrates your failures for the progress that they indicate. Paint a daredevil lightning bolt on your helmet, push off, and leave a trail of face-plants in your wake.

Go, go, go! Leave your picky, persnickety, grammar-fixated, thinky mind in the dust. Move your pen faster than feels comfortable and challenge your overprotective internal Safety Committee that says, "For God's sake, that's so cliché/immature/whiny/arrogant/ignorant/stale/unhip," and on and on. Fly over all the seemingly lethal little objections, right past knowing what you want to say next, into having not a clue what might come out of the pen. Move your pen so fast that you write things that mortify you, things that don't sound like you, and, hopefully, things that surprise you. Blaze past the red pen that your inner critic holds poised, dying to correct your spelling, diagram your sentences, and rate your ideas "pass" or "fail." Too bad, suckah!

Perfect is the
enemy of done.

With any luck, you will put some things down on the page that will make you cringe. Sometimes, speed-writing will cause a Tourette's-like effect, and the things you're most afraid of saying will fly out of your pen. You're not a bad person for having these things in your brain. Everything you've ever experienced or witnessed is in there. It's the big, fabulous, unique storage bin of you. Try approaching this content, this heap of stuff, with the same level of detachment you bring to the neighbor's yard sale.

Your head is crammed with images, stories, memories, worries, recipes, rules, news, gossip, and scraps of songs and TV shows and conversations. When you write something aberrant, there's no need for alarm. It's just a thought. Who knows why it's even in your head? Maybe it came from that episode of *The Sopranos*, maybe it's something you overheard in the grocery-store line, maybe it's a synaptic misfire or a delayed reaction to a long-ago fight-or-flight encounter. Or maybe it's the inspired, near-genius start to the novel you had no idea was in you.

Alternatively, you may be horrified with how tame or boring your speed-writes are. You outrun the censor and all you get is a blow-by-blow of your day or some whining about your relationship woes? This is perfectionism again, wanting to pick up the pebbles and polish them. Notice the impulse and let it go. Your brain and soul may need to expel some clutter before you get to what you want to say.

Our thoughts are just like pebbles: some are shiny, some are sharp, but if you stop to evaluate every single one you'll never get anywhere. Instead, focus on movement and momentum and enjoying the ride. When you look up, you'll see that you've covered an awful lot of ground!

Prompt: Speed-write

In the following exercise, speed is the only thing you're concerned with. *Swoosh! Swoosh!* You're screaming downhill, being chased by a hungry giganotosaurus, with no time to think about style or spelling or what your ass looks like in these pants—you're just trying to stay alive.

Step One: Free fall. With no prompt, no goal, and no idea what will happen, start moving your pen as fast as it will go. Be curious to see what will come out of your pen next. Say "Yes!" to everything that comes into your head and funnel it right through your pen onto the page. Notice the desire to be brilliant, funny, interesting, or at least coherent . . . and shake it off. If you draw a blank, write: *I'm drawing a blank. Shit, there's nothing here. Usually I can't get away from all the junk in my head, and now nothing, nothing, nothing . . .* Eventually, your mind will unclench against the vulnerability and the words will flood back in. Write for six minutes.

Step Two: Speed haiku. Let's step it up a notch. Choose a topic—your spouse, the weather, cheese sandwiches; it doesn't matter—and write five or more haiku exploring your subject. Go for quantity, not quality. This means letting go of beauty, perfection, or even making sense. If your inner perfectionist is horrified by your hasty haiku, good! Let your part wild nature off the leash and get muddy paw prints all over his white carpet and sofa. I mean, who puts a white sofa in a playroom anyway? Write as many haiku as you can in six minutes.

Note: For the uninitiated, a haiku is a form of Japanese poetry that consists of three lines. The first line has five syllables, the second line has seven, and the third line has five. That's *syllables*, not words. A haiku usually doesn't rhyme. It often explores nature, or the seasons, and a master may spend years crafting a single poem—which is why it's perfect for provoking perfectionism.

Bonus Prompts: Other Uses for Speed-writing

Take back the pen. Every time your critic says, "No, no, no," you say, "Yes, yes, yes!" Exercise the "yes muscle" until it's strong enough to compete with the overdeveloped "no muscle." Saying yes is the only way to get to the surprising stuff. If you're choosing and deciding, you're not receiving surprises.

Clear the leaves off the pond. Speed-writing is a great way to empty out the clutter in your head. Think of it as sweeping the leaves off the surface of a pond so you can see into the depths.

Find out what's in your mind. There is so much in there! Your mind is constantly bringing it all in and sorting it without you even consciously participating. If you're aware of it, you can use it in your work.

Pin the monkeys to the page. Do you have a monkey mind? Pin the thoughts to the page so that they aren't swinging from synapse to synapse, chattering and throwing banana peels everywhere.

Break the spell of the blinking cursor. Any time you're slowing down, thinking of a better way to say something, typing two words and then deleting them over and over for twenty minutes, or picking your fingernails clean of polish, jump to pen and paper, set the timer, and blurt-splat the scene or monologue, or whatever it is, onto the page in three minutes. Do this with no idea of what you'll write and no concern for quality. Do it five more times if you have to. Just don't let your pen stop.

Rewire your brain. You're probably not surprised to hear that many of the practices that we adopt to get by in polite society don't serve us in the creative process. That's okay. Our brains are incredibly plastic and adaptive. The practice of speed-writing untangles the snarled wiring that has developed to keep us careful, uncurious, and surprise-free. Speed-writing disables the alarm that sends out troops of uniformed thinkers to examine every tiny pebble for danger while we cling nervously to a tree. If employed regularly, speed-writing gets your wheels turning fast enough that you won't even feel the pebbles.

More Ways to Blow By the Pebbles

- Set your font size to two points, so that you can see the words stacking up but you can't see what you're writing well enough to pick it apart.
- Set the font color to beige, so the words are too faint to read.
- Frame a picture of your biggest hero and put it on your desk. When you get thinky or afraid, look at that person and remember that he or she had flops and failures and false starts, too.
- Remove your Delete key.
- Play music with a fast beat and let it affect your writing rhythm.

* Take some kind of class, like improv, that encourages taking risks and saying yes; this will crack open your writing, too.
* If you have a competitive spirit, write with a friend and race pens.
* Learn to fall well: Talk to someone who scares you. Ask for a favor from someone who might say no. Dance at a party where nobody else is dancing. Look stupid, flail, fall, and survive. Repeat.

5

Worry-Shoulding and Iffing

Live Strawberry to Strawberry

A Zen koan is a small story that poses a problem or riddle with no good answer. It's my understanding that Zen students meditate on them in order to get free of reason and access deeper intuition; I never liked them because they hurt my brain. However, I was recently reminded of one about a monk and a tiger and realized that it speaks perfectly to a common creative issue.

It goes like this—*ahem*: A monk was walking along a path when he noticed a shock of gold out of the corner of his eye. Crouched on a rock, eyeing him hungrily, was a tiger. The monk broke into a run, moving as fast as his sandals would carry him, and the tiger gave chase. Ahead, the monk could see that the earth dropped away—a sheer cliff. Inescapable. But there was a vine! He kept up his pace, shot off the cliff, and grabbed for it. There he hung, dangling from the slender vine, a hungry tiger above him, a deadly drop to sharp rocks below him, and—what was that sound? *Crunch, crunch, crunch.* A mouse was chewing its way through his lifeline. What a predicament. But hello! He noticed a flash of the deepest jewel red, there on the cliff face before him: a wild strawberry growing between two rocks. The monk reached out and plucked the fruit. Popping it into his mouth, he thought, *This is the sweetest thing I've ever tasted.*

Practice #8: Live Strawberry to Strawberry

Sometimes writing feels exactly like hanging from a vine with the violent jaws of regret behind me, the jagged rocks of my unknown future below me, and all the current pressures of life gnawing through my thin tether. In that frame of mind, a strawberry, no matter how perfect, doesn't have a chance with me.

A SHORT LIST OF WRITER WORRIES

- Goals
- Deadlines
- Word count
- Yesterday's writing flowed; today's was sticky—what if I've lost my mojo?
- Can't think of the right word—what if I'm getting Alzheimer's?
- How many rejections are too many?
- What if I get sued for libel?
- I should work on my social media platform.
- I should have done things differently.
- What if I'd had a better mentor or gone to a better school with better connections?
- I should send my work out, try harder to get an agent, work harder on my marketing.
- I should spend more time with my family.
- I should write about something that will change the world.

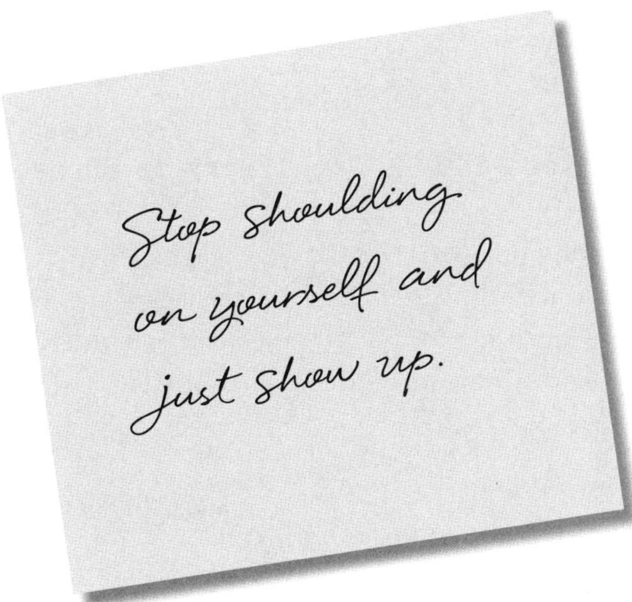

Stop shoulding
on yourself and
just show up.

The past is done, the future is coming in its own time, and we're all gonna die someday. In the meantime, there's something juicy right *here*, and if you give it your full attention, your life will make sense.

The growl of the tiger, the fidelity of the vine, and the painful death on the rocks are compelling, I'll give you that. They seem *really* important. They are big, big worries. But worrying about them won't change them one bit. So what if you take your attention away from these big, big worries and give it, instead, to some small, tasty act of creativity?

Today, all you have to do is a page, a paragraph, a prompt, a really tiny poem. Reach out with your pen and grab what you can. That's it. And that's everything.

One bright red strawberry at a time: that's how you git 'er done.

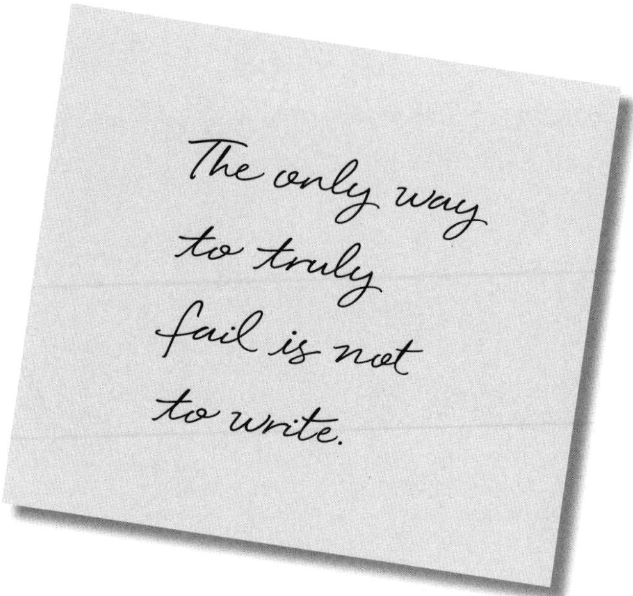

The only way
to truly
fail is not
to write.

Prompt: A Week of Strawberries

Today: Go to the stationery store and buy a new pen. Tasty.

Tomorrow: Write your current favorite word on the back of the receipt with your new pen. Delicious.

Day Three: Find an old, half-used journal, flip to a fresh page, and use that word in a sentence. Ambrosia.

Day Four: Write the sentence that follows that sentence. Notice your hunger to keep writing, and then keep writing. Yum, yum, yum.

Day Five: Notice the character who keeps knocking on the window of your imagination. Open the window. Ask her in. Become ravenous for details, and notice how she opens up in the warmth of your attention. (The details are more fresh strawberries, see? Writing the details down is eating them. Sugar rush!)

Day Six: Read what you've written, underline anything that piques your interest, and write down anything new that comes into your mind. Check the window for other characters. Okay, that's three small things, but in case you're really hungry . . .

Day Seven: Take a walk and let the week's little actions sift through you.

6

Fear—Playing It Safe

Disobey and Investigate

In my second year of acting school, we had worked our way through naturalistic, modern, and experimental theater and now we were edging into the classics. My classmate Jean and I chose the "maid scene" from *The Duchess of Malfi* because it was the least vile option. Jacobean tragedies were a soul-smudging slog through murder, rape, and a startling amount of incest; I just wanted to get through it and get on to Chekhov. The maid scene was just a bit of fluff, supposedly stuck in the play for comic relief. Neither of us was particularly adept at comedy, so we focused on text work and period style.

After performing on scene day, Jean and I turned toward the polite applause of our classmates and teachers and awaited feedback. Jack, the teacher whose good word everybody wanted, took off his thick glasses and rubbed his eyes.

Not a good sign.

"Well . . ." He tossed his curly curtain of hair back so we had a clear view of his sour smile. "Your text work was clearly very *thorough* . . ."

Not a compliment.

"Did anyone tell you that this scene is comedic?" he asked. "What were you two *doing* up there? Bring the scene back next week, and I don't care what you do, just make me laugh."

Jean and I locked ourselves in a rehearsal room and miserably tried to hammer some comedy into the archaic, stiff scene.

"Jesus!" Jean tossed her script on the floor. "I'm not funny, Deb. I'm just not."

"Me neither." I plopped down next to her. "If only there had been a poignant scene."

Jean moaned. "I can do poignant."

"You kill poignant."

"Thanks."

When my roommate, Phil, told me he was coming to scene redo day, I forbade it. "I'm going to die up there, Phil. I can't have you see me like that."

The terror took its toll on my digestive tract, and by the time Jean and I were in costume I was dehydrated and shaking from all the time in the bathroom. Jean was a bad color of gray, even with stage makeup.

The scene involved Jean's character, the duchess, testing a love potion on my character, the maid. The comedy was to be found, we'd guessed, in the effects of the potion, so we'd gone with a Jerry Lewis–level reaction that involved, among other things, me throwing myself into the wall repeatedly and then spinning on the floor à la *The Three Stooges*, going, "Woop, woop, woop!"

I had never experienced stage fright on this level.

"I'm not funny. I've never been funny. Let's just do the scene the old way. We'll restore our good standing in the Chekhov round," I said.

Jean threw down her eyebrow pencil and grabbed me by the face. Her hands were freezing. "We are doing this the way we rehearsed it and we are doing it *balls to the wall. That* is what we are doing."

"Balls to the wall. Got it."

After the scene, I whispered in her ear, "Good job."

"You too."

And we turned, heads bowed, to receive our humiliation. But instead of criticism, there was cacophony. There was so much noise and confusion that it took us a minute to realize that some folks had laughed themselves off their chairs and were still convulsing too hard to climb back on. In the front row, Jack wore a smug smile.

I never heard the end of it from Phil when he found out he'd missed a triumph because of my fear of failure.

Practice #9: Disobey and Investigate

Without Jack's push, I would have obeyed my fear and played it safe. If not for him, I might never have discovered that I was funny. I might have been forever stuck in the narrow territory between poignant and technically rigorous.

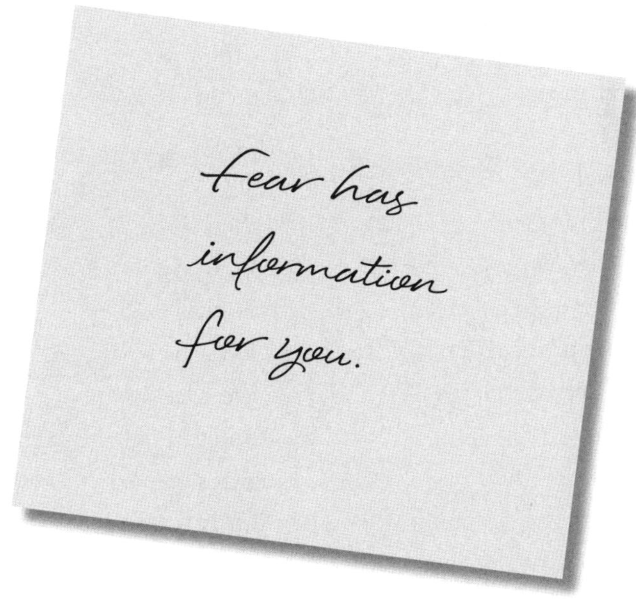
Fear has
information
for you.

Terror and exhilaration are flip sides of the same emotion—they both light up your nervous system to let you know something significant is happening. That significant thing could be life-threatening or life-enhancing, and your nerves can't always distinguish between the two. If we think of fear as a rudimentary alert system, it becomes useful instead of crippling. It alerts us that we're at the outer edge of our known world. Is it the edge of a cliff, or the edge of a great discovery? That's the question, and we love a good question, right? Because it cues our curiosity, and curiosity is stronger than fear.

I had a friend who, when his wife got pregnant, started having a recurring dream that a pack of wolves was chasing him. He ran and ran, hid in Dumpsters, scrambled onto roofs, and jumped into rivers trying to escape them. Finally they drove him to the edge of a steep ravine, where, shaking, crying, he scrambled to decide which death he preferred, falling or mauling. Picking up a rock, he spun around. "Why won't you leave me alone?! Why are you chasing me?!"

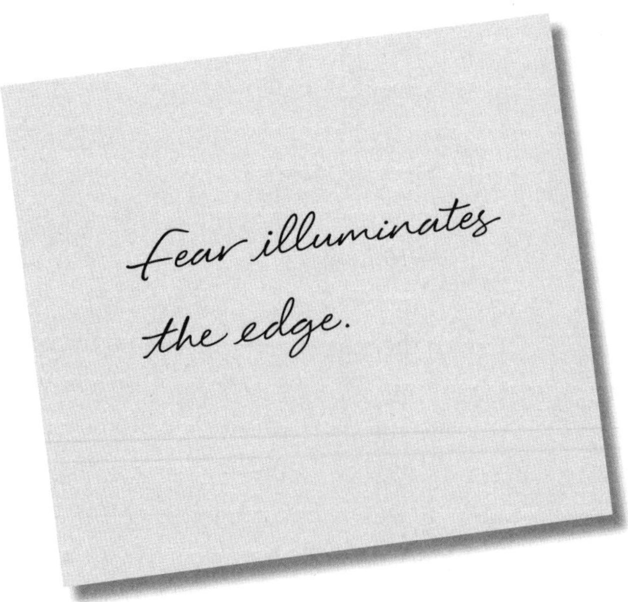
Fear illuminates
the edge.

The wolves skidded to a stop and, to his surprise, one spoke. "We don't chase you. We follow you."

When he turned and questioned his fear, it had good information for him. "It's time to leave the comfort of childhood behind and take up your role as pack leader, buddy."

Fear feels like a bully, but it's more like a built-in nanny—a really nervous one. She Bubble Wraps you against falling, failing, or flailing. She flips out at anything that might hurt you or upset your parents. In the real world, you don't want to flout your nanny. She's a nice lady and she really does know best. In the creative realm, though, you want to figure out what Nanny Fear doesn't want you to do and then check that out. In other words, use her to illuminate the edge. Her eyes keep darting toward the candy drawer she doesn't want you to get into, the door she doesn't want you to open, the lines she wants you to color inside. "Where else would I color?" you ask, watching her eyes. Aha! On the walls and on my sister! Thank you, Nanny Fear!

Don't *obey* your fear. Do *investigate* it. Is it responding to a real threat or scaring you away from a growth-promoting risk? Approach the thing you've been afraid to write and give it a poke with your pen.

Prompt: Illuminate the Edge and Investigate

Step One: Launch from the sentence starter "I'm on the verge of . . ." and see where it takes you. Finish it as many different ways as you can, or follow a thread until it runs out of steam and then launch again. From the obvious to the surprising, write whatever wants to come through your pen. Write for six minutes.

Step Two: Ask your fear what it's afraid of. Yes, that's right, just ask it. *What are you afraid will happen if I write or audition or run for* *office or become a comedian? What are you protecting me from? What is the worst-case scenario?* Let your fear answer through your pen. If it helps to visualize a nanny (or a wolf), go for it. Sit her down, give her a cup of tea, and get her talking. Take dictation for six minutes as she explains why you need protection and what she's protecting you from.

Step Three: Read back through your writing and underline those things that can be shifted from "red alert" to "investigate." When fear detects a danger, it wants us to run in the opposite direction without hesitation and without question. Exercises such as the ones I offer here are designed to help you slow down the process so you can get a good look at the "threat" and make an informed decision about whether to engage or hightail it.

7

Boredom—Where Did the Love Go?

Kick It Up a Notch

For about six years, my husband and I ran a theater in Ojai, California. We put up some shows that I will be forever proud of, grew enormously, and made lifelong friends with some of the best people on earth, but the workload was often bone crushing.

Chris and I weren't married then, but we might as well have been. After a few years of producing shows, teaching, raising money, and being run off our feet, being attractive or exciting to each other just wasn't a priority or even a possibility. I never caught him looking at me with the kind of relish he used to, and tired and busy as I was, I didn't particularly crave to be relished, anyway.

Meanwhile, we'd added a new singing workshop to the schedule, and it was my job to audit it. We didn't put our students through anything we weren't willing to do ourselves, and since I don't sing in the car or even in the shower, I had to find the willingness to step up and perform in the mandatory showcase.

I ended up missing most of the classes because of the never-ending string of theatrical emergencies I had to deal with. To make things worse, I chose the song "River" by Joni Mitchell, not realizing how high its high note actually was. It didn't sound high when Joni did it. It turned out I could only hit it about a third of the time. The rest of the time, my voice slipped its track and became a whisper-scream. I got through the performance, but I crashed on the high note. Nobody threw rotten fruit, though, and I was just glad not to have to juggle the class anymore. Back to work.

After the show, Chris hung back until the initial post-show excitement had died down, and when he approached me, I saw that his eyes where shining. He'd been crying—he still was, a little. He put a glass of wine in my hand and whispered in my ear, "You were so beautiful up there." He told me later that he'd been so moved that he'd had to leave the theater after my song so as not to disturb the people around him with his weeping.

Chris had been reintroduced to a part of me he hadn't seen in a while. The dusty, everyday, set-painting, campaign-planning, show-producing, donor-schmoozing, computer-screen-staring hull fell away to reveal the crackling, uncomfortably awake risk-taker underneath, and the result was the eradication of boredom and an infusion of relishing.

Practice #10: Kick It Up a Notch

There are times when you want to spend every waking moment writing and creating. It's like the infatuation stage of a relationship; there is a feeling that you will never come to the end of your ravenous desire to explore. You'll go wherever your pen wishes to take you—to alternate realities, into your haunted past, straight into the heart of danger. You work through meals, you work through the night, but it never feels like work. Then one day, the love is just . . . gone. You'd rather go to the dentist than write. How can such a powerful attraction just dry up?

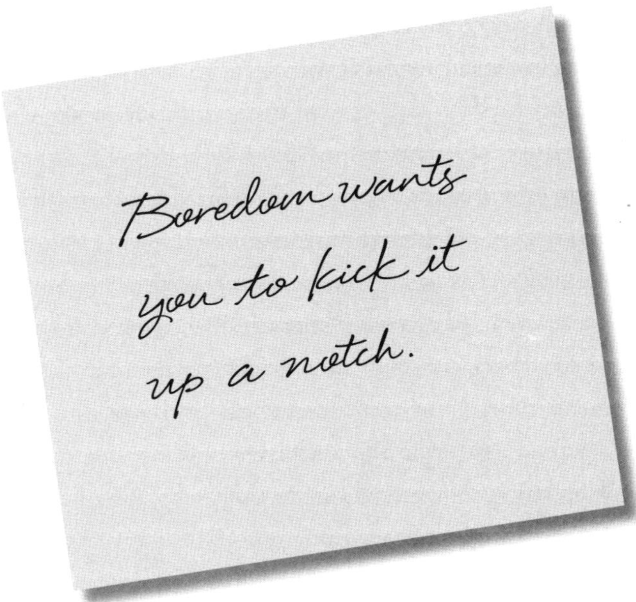

Boredom wants
you to kick it
up a notch.

Familiarity can breed contempt—but only when we misunderstand boredom's purpose. Boredom is there to make you feel restless. When you've been hanging around in known territory too long, boredom arrives to let you know you're not being challenged by or finding meaning in what you're doing.

We can't tolerate stagnation for too long, and that's a good thing. If our species was okay with the same old same old, we'd never have invented the wheel or stood upright or tried cooking our food. We naturally crave growth, whether or not we enjoy the experiences that cause it.

Unfortunately, new challenges and growth experiences aren't always the first thing we reach for to relieve the discomfort of boredom. Social media or shopping or a pint of rocky road might provide enough stimulus to scratch the itch of restlessness.

Another way to relieve boredom is to light those little fires of drama that we talked about earlier—to pick fights, indulge outrage, or nudge sleeping dogs. These unconscious reactions to boredom can create enough excitement to temporarily relieve our restlessness, but they don't address its root cause.

If we let it, boredom can be a real friend, pushing us to go deeper or to get more ambitious with our exploration. Monks and other ascetics make their world as stark as possible—living in cells, restricting their speech, disavowing personal possessions—all in an effort to starve the mind into a higher state of consciousness. When boredom isn't appeased with our regular, go-to stimuli, it prompts us to look deeper.

It's no surprise that one of the stereotypical images of boredom is that of the daydreamer: while the teacher drones on with tired rhetoric, the daydreaming student stares out the window, engaged in a charged exploration of far-flung worlds or her own internal multiverse. Daydreaming is one of our most powerful tools for taking things to the next level. It's in the daydreaming state that we have our biggest "Eureka!" moments.

Boredom drives our most basic human mandate—to explore and innovate. You never see a bored baby. They are in the grip of exploration every minute, discovering the laws of physics and probing the world's minutiae with the fullness of their five senses.

If you've lost that lovin' feeling toward a project that once had you in the grip of desire, try pushing off from the boredom toward the next level of what you're working on.

Prompt: Push Off of Boredom

Boredom is a sign that you've gotten too comfortable. Since we spend so much of our time trying to *get* comfortable, it might be tempting to just ignore that restlessness or appease it with some temporary fix. However, once you know that this little itch you're feeling is a sign that you're ready to go to the next level in your work, you can go ahead and get excited.

Unfortunately, boredom only provides the impetus to reach for something more. It doesn't tell you what the "more" is. Here are some exercises that explore the "more" beyond your comfort zone.

Step One: Make two lists.

1. "Things I Would/Will Never Do." Get everything on the page that you consider to be out of bounds, off limits, or out of character for you. If it's easier, just finish the sentence, "I would never . . ." as many different ways as you can, from the obvious to the shocking to the embarrassing: *I would never spit on another person*; *I would never eat a bug*; *I will never forgive my sister*; *I will never find the courage to ask that girl out*. List for six minutes.

   Read through your list and underline the things that have a little heat around them. Choose one to explore, and entertain the notion of doing that thing you would never do. Write about what it would be like for six minutes.
2. "Things I Would Do in a Second, Given Half a Chance." All limitations are removed—fear, time, responsibility, morality, the laws of physics—and the sky is the limit. Really let it rip. Reach for all those unrealistic, impractical fantasies: travel, love, adventure, achievement. Maybe you would learn trapeze, start your own circus, marry a certain movie star, sit down with a certain world leader. Maybe you would *become* a world leader. Don't try to be deep. Write the exhilarating and the ridiculous. Write for six minutes.

   Read through your list and underline the things that have some energy to them. Choose one that's good and charged and write about what it would be like if you got the chance to do that thing. Write for six minutes.

Step Two: Say it.

1. Launch from the sentence starter "What I really want to say is . . ." and see where it takes you. What do you really want to say through your work? What is pushing to get out through

your pen or your paintbrush? What do you *really* want to express through your body or your lens or your guitar? You can finish the sentence a hundred different ways, or you might hook into something and follow it until it loses steam and then start again from "What I really want to say is . . ." Write for six minutes.

2. Ask your story or your project or your very soul, "What do you really want to say?" Ask this question humbly and earnestly and with great curiosity and then get ready to receive the answer through your pen. If you've never entered into dialogue with your work before, it might feel a little strange or even contrived. That's okay. It doesn't have to feel like an electric connection to be effective. If it feels like you're forcing it, that's fine, and it won't work against the exercise in the least. Just ask the question and then take dictation. Write for six minutes.

Bonus Prompts: Other Ways to Push Off of Boredom

Find someone who knows more than you do about your subject matter and interview them. Extra points if you find them intimidating.

Invent an imaginary expert or practitioner who knows more than you do about your subject and "interview" him or her.

Make your character do something that scares her. If you don't know what this might be, have her make a list of "Things I Would Never Do," and then choose one and have her do it.

Have your character finish the sentence "I want to explore . . ." for five minutes. Look into the things that exist beyond her known world.

Take a break from your protagonist and become curious about your antagonist (or any secondary character). Spend time with him. Let him take you on a tour of his house. Find out something you didn't know about him. What bores him? What's the most challenging thing he's ever done?

Have you ever noticed a stranger looking at the person you love with real interest or attraction? Doesn't it freshen your own attraction real quick? Pretend you've run into someone who's just leaving your study and they look a little weak in the knees. "I just ran across the most amazing piece of writing in there," they tell you. "I'll never be the same. Man, how I wish I'd written it." Now go read your work and try to see it through their eyes.

8

Expectation-Cursing the Gods

Channel Hercules / Know What You Are Fighting For

Of all Zeus's illegitimate children, his wife, Hera, hated Hercules the most. It could have been because Hercules's mother was the most brilliant and beautiful woman alive, but more likely it was that little matter of Zeus putting the infant Hercules to Hera's breast as she slept, stealing food from her own children in order to give the bastard brat an extra dose of strength and immortality.

It was probably this betrayal that inspired Hera to new heights of cruelty. She found opportunities to bother and bedevil Hercules all along the way, but she waited until he was a husband and father to work her worst. At his moment of greatest contentment, with epic accomplishments behind him and a gratifying future before him, she touched his mind with a terrible madness, causing him to slaughter his wife and children in a blind rage.

When Hercules woke to this gruesome scene, it didn't matter that he'd not been in his right mind; the heartbreak and guilt burdened him with a pain unlike any he'd ever experienced in war. It was not a pain he knew how to bear or a wound he knew how to heal.

Wretched, he went to his father and asked how he might endure living in the grip of this crushing sorrow. Zeus sent him to the oracle, who pronounced that if Hercules would submit himself to King Eurystheus and do whatever he commanded, he would have his redemption.

Hercules *hated* King Eurystheus, whom he knew to be a vain and frivolous man who had never been to battle himself but sent other men to fight his wars. Nonetheless, Hercules went to the king, bent his knee, bowed his head, and asked for his penance.

King Eurystheus devised ten labors for Hercules, none of which he expected Hercules to survive. Hercules wrestled enchanted lions and many-headed snakes. He returned with trophies and boons to lay at the feet of a begrudging Eurystheus and then went back for more. When Hercules completed all ten labors, the king disqualified two on technicalities and added two more.

I like to imagine that moment when Hercules is truly on the other side of his trials and his suffering is relieved. There will be no parade or feast, as there had been when he returned, scarred but victorious, from a battle. There will be no medal of valor, no wagon full of gold. There will be just the peace and the wholeness of redemption.

Practice #11: Channel Hercules

There are moments when this work seems impossible, when I despair. There are times when writing feels like being blindfolded and tossed into a room packed with objects, and I'm not only supposed to name them all but figure out how they fit together. At those times, I think of my man Hercules.

What I take from the Hercules myth is that when it comes to the work of the soul—redemption, creation, transformation—there are strenuous processes that we must submit to, that this is the way it has always been, and that, though difficult, the process is necessary and the rewards will be great.

In the creative process, as in any transformative process, you may feel you've been tricked and cursed by the gods. You may face and fight monsters both internal and external. It will probably feel unfair. Your good intentions and past achievements may not be taken into account. It will almost certainly take longer than you think it should and ask more of you than feels reasonable. You'll likely feel as though you have no control, and that those who *do* have control are insensitive to your anguish.

That's not to say that there won't be periods of ease, revelation, and even elation. There will be victories of varying magnitude along the way. I think of Hercules pitting his strength and wit against this variety of foes and know there were times when he felt he'd used his skills to the fullest or reached deep and gone beyond what he thought he was capable of.

The Hercules myth reveals three truths about the creative process:

1. It is going to test your mettle.
2. You are inherently designed to persevere.
3. If you persevere you will be enlarged by the process, not diminished.

There really are no shortcuts to creating. It takes as long as it takes. When you finish your first draft, there's always that secret hope that you'll be told, "It's a work of genius! Well done! Here's a colossal amount of money!" But instead, the rewrite awaits, or the next project or deadline. Somehow, even though you know this, it still hits you like a punch to the gut every time.

We've all heard tales of artists who receive their creations fully formed, as though a muse is just using them like a kind of Etch A Sketch. I'm sure it happens, but I'm willing to bet that in most cases, these artists experienced a frustrating fallow period beforehand, while their subconscious minds were milling the coming creation. It's just extremely rare, if it happens at all, for creation to occur in a just-add-water fashion. We all want to be that rare person, that winner of the creative lottery. But the problem with expecting to win the lottery is that it disincentivizes you from doing the work.

Hercules was a bona fide battle-tested hero with Olympian blood in his veins. He might have expected his labors to be a cakewalk, but he knew that none of his previous combat experience could prepare him to fight a three-headed hellhound. All he could do was get his head in the game and be ready for anything.

Hercules knew it was possible to survive the labors, even if only just barely. He was heartbroken and crippled by remorse and grief, but he was also experienced, strong, and resourceful, and he had been assured by the oracle that if he gave it his all, it would be possible to come through and earn his redemption.

Trade expectation
for optimism.

The ability to envision a good outcome is essential to the creative process. In order to enter the creative process and give it what's required, you must be able to imagine the possibility of successfully completing whatever it is you wish to make.

You must be clear with yourself, at the beginning and all the way through, that whatever it takes, you're up to it. And I assure you that you are. Because unlike fighting mythical monsters, creation is an endeavor we humans are designed for. Making and raising a child is a creative act of mind-boggling complexity and massively high stakes, yet humans undertake it daily because we're built for it. And if we have respect for the process and are optimistic about the outcome, the result can be profound.

Practice #12: Know What You Are Fighting For

Another expectation that can suck the marrow out of your creative bones is the anticipation of a reward that will justify the effort.

First of all, there is no reward commensurate with the soul effort it takes to distill the value from life's heartbreak and let it become the beating heart of a screenplay or a sculpture or a symphony. There is no value system by which we could determine the amount of money or fame or critical success that would properly compensate the creation of something new in the world, whether it's a novel or a polio vaccine or a child.

Hercules knew he couldn't live the rest of his life with so much pain in his heart, and he knew that, at the end of the labors, he would be relieved of it. This is what he was fighting for. Not gold. Not his due respect from King Eurystheus. Not revenge. The transformation of his suffering and the forgiveness of his debt were the reward.

They don't call it a "heroic effort" for nothin'.

King Eurystheus dictated the labors to Hercules from the safety and comfort of his throne. He didn't have to lift a finger or shed one drop of sweat over any of it as he lined his halls with the pelts of magical monsters. He risked nothing and enjoyed the spoils of another's labor. There are King Eurystheuses in the creative world as well—people who lack an understanding of, or respect for, the creative process but still aim to profit from it.

It does you no good to wish these folks ill or to wish the world worked differently. Be like Hercules. Show up with everything you've got, stay in it as long as it takes, and pursue the value that can only be redeemed through the creative process. It will feel like a heroic effort because that's exactly what it is.

That's why odes about Hercules have survived the centuries, and why you've never, ever heard of King Eurystheus until now.

II

The Nature versus Nurture of Resistance

Trading What You've Been Taught for What's True

It's in our nature to be creative. We see this in the way that all children play-act, paint, dance, and sing without fear, as though they were born to it. But at some point the creative spirit is "nurtured" right out of us. Parenting, education, peers, and pressures converge and conspire with our need to belong and be safe, introducing doubt and even shame. It's like pouring sugar into a gas tank. The conventional wisdom has been that these ghosts in the machine must be approached therapeutically, emotionally, or psychologically. But what happens if we leverage our naturally occurring creativity instead?

9

Time-Hoops and To-dos

Get a Healthy Sense of Entitlement / Come Out as Creative / Tame the Temptations / Take Down the Tower

For the first few years we lived together, I nursed a continual resentment toward Chris's "I'll get to it" attitude about his share of the household chores. To tell you the truth, it was almost a deal breaker. I would watch him reading a book or flipping through sports channels as I canned the mountain of vegetables from the garden so they wouldn't go to waste, and I'd seethe. I couldn't scrape together thirty minutes for my writing, but he had time to *idle*.

I didn't want to nag, so I'd hold it in. But I didn't want to be a passive-aggressive martyr, either, so I'd wait until my feelings built up and then I'd confront him: "I don't get how—I mean, if you *love* me—how can you let me clean the bathroom when it's *your* job?"

"Don't clean it, then," he'd say. "I'll get to it."

"Chris, it's furry. And you could do the dishes once in a while."

"Why do we have eight of everything if not to buy us time between washing dishes?"

Grrr! I thought of withholding sex, but was I really going to whore myself out for help around the house?

I had a recurring fantasy about what crime I might commit to get myself thrown in a minimum-security prison so I could write. Teaching, marketing my workshops, building a website, answering e-mails from panicked writers—that all had to get done. The garden had to be tended, the dog had to be walked, my mother had to be taken to the doctor. Then there was the little matter of the theater we were running. I was tired and raw, and the stain around the toilet bowl made me want to sob. Could someone please shut me in a cell for eight hours a day and shoot me if I tried to escape? (Because of course I'd try to escape. If there was a to-do to be done anywhere in the world, I'd feel compelled to do it.)

One day I was racing to a meeting, eyebrows knit, a pulsing knot of stress in my chest, and NPR on the car radio. Someone was railing about the Second Amendment and how to interpret the Bill of Rights. I shoved in a CD to shut them up, but it was too late. I began to daydream about a guy named Bill O'Rights, feet up on the dashboard, coffee mug steaming, gazing out the window, obnoxiously content.

"Typical," I snorted.

He raised an eyebrow at me. "I have a right to my downtime."

"Yeah—what about *my* rights?"

"What about them?"

"You're hogging them all, you entitled schmuck."

He shook his head and chuckled. "I can't take your rights, lady. You gave them all away."

I pulled over and put my forehead on the wheel, exhausted and sad. The truth was unavoidable: I had entitlement envy. I wanted to revoke Chris's (and everybody else's) right to relax, expand, and self-express because my own bill of rights didn't have any of that stuff in it.

And Bill O'Rights was right. There would never be a moment

when I felt I'd done enough to earn my writing time. There would always be more dirt to clean, more money to make, more needs to meet. Was I really going to devote my life to a Sisyphean battle with disorder and dirt? Was this to be my contribution to the world—a fully ticked to-do list?

If I was honest, I knew that as a living creature I was encoded with an inalienable right to enrichment, rest, and, yes, even pleasure. It didn't have to be earned; it was just a part of the basic package. More urgently, I was inviolably entitled to do my true work, to write and create stories. It was a biological imperative. For me, it was the equivalent of a fertility clock going off, shrill and insistent.

It came to me then that I was already in prison: I had bricked myself into a tower of unrelenting responsibilities. It didn't matter if Chris pitched in; I would always find more to do. And so began the painstaking process of dismantling the tower.

Practice #13: Get a Healthy Sense of Entitlement

I was taught that entitlement is a dirty word and that we prove our worth through work, service, and accomplishments. I have long felt the outrageous untruth of this idea, and still I've been driven by it—thinking that we're rewarded for saving, accumulating, stretching ourselves thin, and sacrificing, and there are bonus points for making it all look easy.

There is no committee that can determine when you've worked hard enough, done enough good, or earned enough money to be entitled to some creative time. And anyway, in our world as it's currently configured, enough is never enough. Nope, your inalienable entitlements can't be awarded or earned, because you already have them. They have to be *owned*.

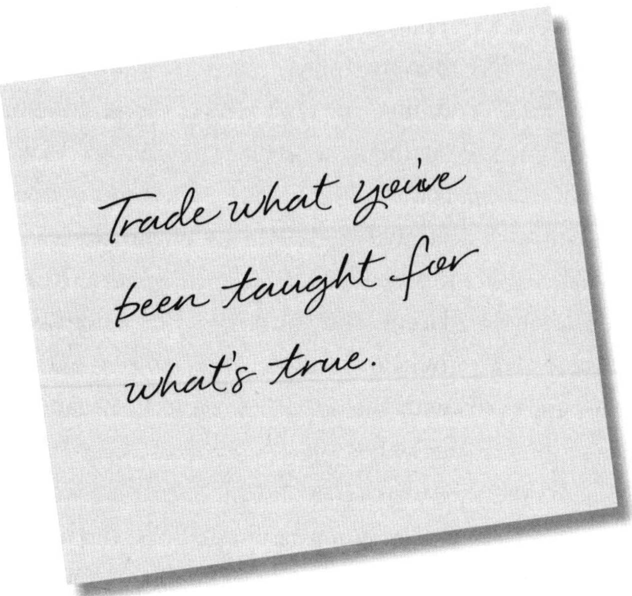

Trade what you've
been taught for
what's true.

You are entitled to some things simply by virtue of being a human on this earth. Here are some of those things:

* Nourishment
* Proper shelter
* Kindness
* A good night's sleep
* Time in nature
* Playtime
* And most important of all, *time to create*

A healthy sense of entitlement doesn't happen overnight. I'll admit to being a hard case, and I often backslide into old habits. To be honest, it sometimes feels safer to work myself down to a nub than it does to do my real work, for all sorts of reasons, most of which are addressed in this book. Rebuilding your bill of rights is a process and it can take time.

Look, it's not about putting your tiny princess feet up on a pillow. It's not about being owed anything for fulfilling your creative destiny. It's not even about inner peace or self-actualization.

Okay, then what *is* it about, smarty?

It's about *creating* something of value, rather than proving your value or accumulating things of value.

Why do you think we call that God person "the Creator"? On some deep level, we all know that the best way to honor this one precious life we've been given, and the consciousness that goes with it, is to create—not to die with the most toys, the most organized closet, or the lowest percentage of body fat.

Recovery hasn't been easy, but with Chris's help I've made great strides. Instead of daily vacuuming the dog hair off the couches, I cover the cushions with old sheets and wash them occasionally. I keep the phone's ringer on silent and return calls when my work is finished. I've let the garden go to seed, deciding that shopping at the farmer's market is virtuous enough. I'm working on developing dust blindness. Basically, I've relearned how to discern between something that's worth doing and something that's a hoop I feel I have to jump through.

You're here
to create, not
accumulate.

Prompt: Know Your Rights

Step One: Launch from the sentence starter "I'm entitled to . . ." and finish it as many different ways as you can. Be sassy. This is not the place to be considerate or tentative. *I'm entitled to eavesdrop on strangers and put them in my story. I'm entitled to spend the whole party writing in a corner, to eat chocolate, to get a hammock for reading and daydreaming.* Write for six minutes.

Step Two: Launch from the sentence starter "If I don't write . . ." (or "paint," or "dance"—choose your medium) and finish it as many different ways as you can. You have permission to be honest, to rave, to be melodramatic. *If I don't write I'll go crazy. If I don't write it, nobody else will.* Move your pen fast for six minutes.

Step Three: Brainstorm your Creative Bill of Rights. Be silly, serious, unrealistic, and impractical. Let it rip. List all the basic and not-so-basic rights that should be recognized as not only inalienable, but intrinsic to creative people. *The right to life, liberty, and sleeping in so as not to miss those drowsy morning insights. The right to wear earbuds and lock the door, yea, even if it means my six-year-old will have to wait until dinner to tell me a joke.*

* Read over your Bill of Rights brainstorm and underline anything you feel drawn to for any reason. Use these underlined items as fodder for a first draft of your personal Creative Bill of Rights.
* Post your Creative Bill of Rights draft above your work area. Refine it and add to it whenever you are called to do so.

Practice #14: Come Out as Creative

Those who don't champion your right to write probably don't know any better, and if they don't know any better it could be that they don't have the inside scoop. It may be time to come out to them as creative.

There is an unexamined and automatic belief, especially among women (ladies, we need to own this), that creativity is self-centered and selfish. Perhaps we believe this because it takes us away from our families or because it can be so emotionally and intellectually consuming. So we attempt to honor our loved ones by putting creativity in the closet. It gets the smallest sliver of us so that the most generous slice can go to the tribe.

We have this all backward. Those who value you value your happiness. They have a personal stake in your well-being because it directly affects their own well-being. If you are stifled or pining or resentful, your loved ones do not benefit at all. If creating is what makes you feel alive and on fire, I promise, they will want that for you.

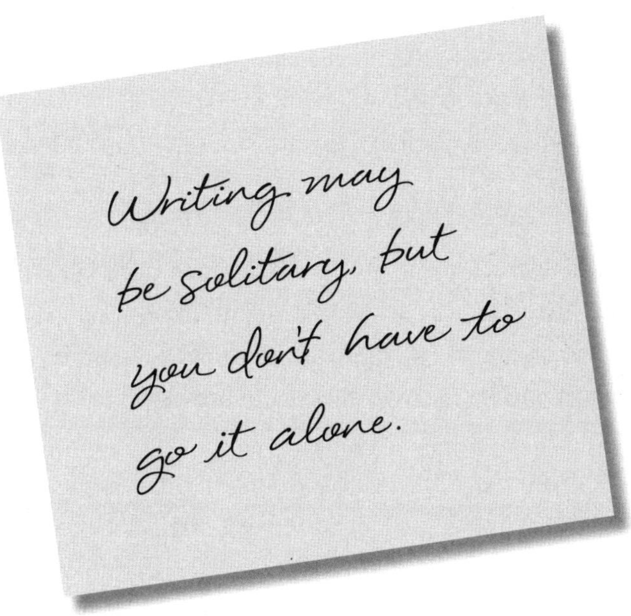

Writing may
be solitary, but
you don't have to
go it alone.

Spouses, children, friends, and even bosses and coworkers are often surprisingly grateful when you tell them precisely how best to support you. And inviting them to do the same has the potential to revolutionize your relationships. For instance, when I confessed to Chris that my dream was to reduce life to "writing, working, and walking—preferably in nature," we moved to a remote cabin in the woods not four months later, and I transitioned my clients to Skype. While he isn't inspired to fight for my right to a spotless house, it turns out Chris is a fierce advocate of my right to write.

Okay, so maybe you're ready to declare your creativity and educate your inner circle about how best to support you, but you don't know how to put it. No problem—I have prepared this sample script to get you started:

> The time I spend creating makes me a better person, friend, parent, and partner. It gives me a way to understand the world and myself that I can't duplicate through any other activity. I know that you care about my well-being and I can't be well if I don't put my creativity at the center of my life, so I hope you'll support my creativity as a way to support me. Here are some things you can do that would make a big difference . . .

Maybe they won't completely understand what creating means to you or what the process involves, but that needn't stop them from having your back. However, if you come out as creative to somebody in your life and they persist in trivializing your writing, it's really no different from someone chiding you for taking breathing so seriously. In that case, do whatever you would do with someone who belittles an essential part of you.

No amount of fashion or facials can give you the glow you get when you're living the fullness of your creative intention. You know it's true. Even if the work is arduous, you're more alive when you're engaged in it. In addition, the creative process places demands on you that cause you to grow. So if you're creating, you're becoming smarter, deeper, and more interesting, and that's a plus for anyone who loves you. Proclaiming your creativity is just another way of reprioritizing toward your true potential.

Tell the most important people in your life that you're done living in the pain of not creating and so you are putting creativity at the very center of your existence. Make sure they understand that if your creativity is at the center of your existence, you will be much more enjoyable to live with.

Prompt: Come Out, Come Out

Step One: Blurt onto the page all the pent-up, passionate, wild words you never felt you could say to anyone, much less your loved ones, about your wish to devote yourself to your creative work. Let it be emotional. Express the pain of deferring your creative projects. Write down what it feels like when you do take your creative space. You can burn it afterward if you like, but for six minutes, just let it rip.

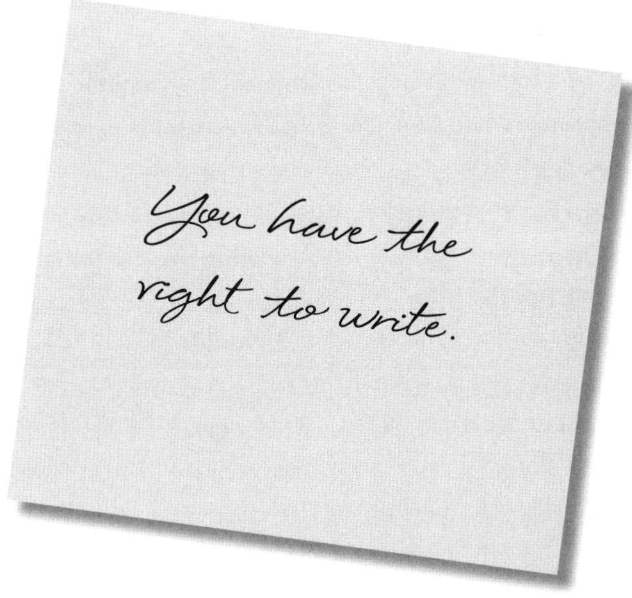
You have the
right to write.

Step Two: Read back through the above brainstorming exercise and underline anything that feels remotely close to what you really want to say to your inner circle about being a creative person and how they can best support you.

Step Three: Use the underlined bits as a starting place for your coming-out speech. Start rough and refine toward a workable draft. Rewrite and edit it until it feels like what you want to say.

Step Four: Read the speech through and take it in. Hear it and become willing to publicly honor your creativity.

Step Five: Read the speech to those people in your life that you'd like to "get real" with and be ready to answer any questions they have.

Practice #15: Tame the Temptations

Your home environment, especially if it's also your work environment, can wear you down with its to-do triggers. If you're home, you're going to want to organize that drawer and spend all day on the phone straightening things out with the insurance company. Here are some ways to remove yourself from temptation:

Go to a café, or any place that's temperature-controlled and writer-friendly, where a warm beverage is made for you instead of by you, and where you don't have to wash your own cup. Lots of natural light is a plus. Hint: Buy something and tip generously. In order to keep from getting sugar- or caffeine-frazzled, make it a mission to sample a new tea with every visit.

Rent a room or office away from home to write in. If you have a dog, make sure dogs are welcome. If your dog is a needy, barking ball of distraction, make sure he has lots of chew toys and leave him at home. Hint: don't fill your "away space" with furniture that must be dusted or plants that must be watered.

Drive to a public park and pull into a parking space with an agreeable view. Move to the passenger seat if you need elbow room. Turn off your phone and put it in the glove box. Write. This works especially well if you have an interval between work and picking the kids up from piano practice. Hint: if you are a man, make sure your car is not pointed toward a playground.

If leaving the house isn't an option, make or buy a "Back at . . ." sign. You've seen these on the doors of shops in small towns—it has a clock face with moveable hands so that when the shopkeepers go to lunch at noon, they can set the hands to show that they'll be back at 1:00 p.m. Put one on your office door to let family members or housemates know when you plan to emerge from your writing session. Let it be known that you don't exist for them while "on the clock." If you don't have a door, hang the sign from the back of your chair.

As another alternative to leaving the house, use to-dos as a reward. Allow yourself five minutes of vacuuming for every forty-five minutes of writing. Tell yourself you can organize one drawer if you write for two days in a row. This way, instead of working on you, the to-dos are working for you.

Practice #16: Take Down the Tower

It's important that you don't attempt to dismantle your tower of to-dos overnight. Undo it brick by brick so that you don't end up buried under the rubble. Limit yourself to one thing a week. Choose a day—One-Thing Thursday, for instance—and on that day free yourself from one to-do, obligation, or object. Be strict—choose only *one* thing.

One thing a week is doable. Your life becomes steadily simpler, and you're not putting off writing for a wall-to-wall decluttering campaign. Eventually, you can up it to two things, and then three, but watch out for that manic part of you that wants to make it a project or squeeze a sense of achievement out of it (because that's just what you need: another lofty goal).

Some One-Thing Thursday activities:

- Give away one potted plant.
- Unsubscribe from one newsletter.
- Delegate one task to a coworker or family member.
- Bow out of book club.
- Forgive someone.
- Let go of a tradition that you no longer enjoy.
- Break up with a frenemy.
- Decide to like the colors in your bathroom for now.
- Tape a "Free" sign to something and put it on the sidewalk.

For me, dismantling the tower meant learning to live with less—less activity; less living space; fewer belongings, clothes, and obligations—and to love what I had left. I started by getting rid of anything nonessential, and then I targeted things that required maintenance. Inaction can also be a powerful tool; I let leaves pile up, cleaned only for company, and allowed my wardrobe to go out of date.

Because you can't be expected to rearrange your life and revolutionize your relationship with your creativity instantly, be kind to yourself: a creative life doesn't have to be an all-or-nothing proposal. You don't have to quit your job or leave your family or sell your house or move to New York City or banish yourself to the woods. You don't have to ditch your responsible self to honor your artistic self. They are the same person; they just need to be better integrated. As you slowly dismantle the tower, you reveal and revive the writer.

While you do your due diligence on the dismantling process, try this: create a pocket in your heart, safe and separate from the everyday stuff—the conflicts, the kids, the parents, the uphill battles and impossible odds. Put a piece of what you're working on in that pocket. It might be a question, a character, a color, a word . . . You can slip a hand into that pocket whenever you want and touch the little treasure that is your story or your novel or your memoir. This way, when you come back to it, it's familiar and welcoming and still warm from your touch. It's like keeping an ember at the ready so it's easier to start the fire the next time.

Prompt: Brick by Brick

Step One: Make a list of your household duties: garbage detail, lawn maintenance, bill paying, kid chauffeuring, laundry. Put absolutely everything on there, from key-for-survival to maddeningly meaningless. Write for as long as it takes.

Step Two: Read back over the list and underline anything:

1. Nonessential—i.e., if you stop doing it no one will come to harm and no crucial systems will break down. For instance, making your bed or your kids' beds; collecting stray shoes and returning them to closets; trimming the hedges to geometrical perfection.
2. Transferable—i.e., it doesn't require your personal touch and could be done by someone else. For instance, everyone can do his or her own laundry; your husband can make dinner on the grill twice a week; your grown-up, live-in son can take over the vacuuming.

Step Three: Look through what you underlined in step two and choose at least two nonessential and two transferable items and add them to your One-Thing Thursday list for future elimination or re-assignment. But remember: Once you give them away, they're *gone.* Resist the urge to take them back when you don't think they're being done properly.

10

Memory-Swiss-cheese Mind

Change Your Mind about Memory / Get Trigger-happy

I had an acting teacher who gave a class in faking emotions. It involved things like staring into a light or irritating your nostril with a Q-tip in order to get some tears going. Though we all rolled our eyes, his point was well taken: Whether or not you're "feeling it," you still have to get the job done. You can't just hang the story out to dry because you can't call up a genuine feeling.

Of course, organic emotion was the ideal. The best way to get to emotion was to find a specific "trigger" to pull it up. For instance, I had only to recall the smell of turpentine to feel a wave of sadness because it was in my great-grandmother's painting studio that I saw the first signs of her dementia. That's what we were going for. Tears that push their way out, joy that makes your feet dance, anger that makes your pulse jump. It was that last one—anger—that gave me the most trouble. And that was fine, until we got to the Greeks.

I was to play Medea. I was twenty-one years old, with exactly zero experience of jealous outrage. Or outrage of any kind. It just wasn't in my inventory. So my Medea was pretty limp. My scene partner did his best to provoke me, playing Jason with an aggravating combination of sensitivity and swagger, but nothing organic was happening, and the "faking it" class hadn't covered the kind of fury that would lead to infanticide.

Meanwhile, a bunch of us went to a new restaurant that served authentic Southern cuisine. I was raised on fried chicken, white gravy, and okra, so I led the charge, looking for the fatty, salty crunch of Grandma Norton's kitchen. Maybe they'd have buttermilk biscuits! My entrée was served with collards, one of the house specialties, but many at the table found collards too challenging and ordered the alternate side dish, succotash. Now, succotash was something I never expected to encounter again in my lifetime—something that, as far as I knew, existed nowhere outside the most nightmarish moments of my childhood, something that contained . . . *lima beans.*

As a small child, I ate everything that was put before me without objection except those disgusting, pale, wrinkled . . . oh, God. To me, they didn't taste remotely like anything I should put in my mouth. They tasted exactly like dollops of wet eraser dust wrapped in toilet paper. Or boogers. Also wrapped in toilet paper. Take your pick. Looking at them there, on the neighboring plates, the flavor appeared in my mouth unbidden.

When served succotash as a child, I would eat all the cubed carrots, corn niblets, and peas, and then try to hide the twelve or so lima beans that remained under some chicken bones or potato skins. But they would invariably draw the unwanted attention of my stepfather, who simply could not abide a child who did not clear her plate of the food he worked so hard to provide. A contest of wills would ensue, sometimes lasting long past *Little House on the Prairie*, by which time the lima beans would be ice cold. He would always win, and I would always end up eating the small pile of ice-cold, bug-colored booger beans.

At twenty-one, these recollections, like most of my memories, had been stored at the back corner of my brain where I wouldn't trip over them. But the sight of the succotash brought them screaming back, and I felt so much revulsion and hatred that I had to turn away.

The next time we rehearsed Medea, all I had to do was think of lima beans and the howl of impotent rage, the sense of injustice, the humiliation, and the surprisingly violent fantasies of righteous revenge were *right there.*

Practice #17: Change Your Mind about Memory

I have a terrible memory—long-term, short-term, mid-term, it's all pretty sketchy. I know a lot of people say that, but I really do. Those who are miffed that I don't find them important enough to remember their names might be comforted to know that I can't remember lots of things that should be important to me: major life events, milestones, catastrophes, achievements, and moments of epic beauty. I used to worry that it was something wrong with my brain—plaques, a tumor, a degenerative disease—and it would get worse and worse until I was like my great-grandma, with no idea who I or anybody else was. (I can catastrophize with the best of them.) I also wondered if this was a massive limitation on my writing. I mean, if I can't remember anything, what am I going to write about? And if I write what I remember, how will I know if it's true? So it was a relief to stumble upon a different way of thinking about memory.

I was in the nanotech department at UC Santa Barbara with four other actors, a director, several media engineers, and a neuroscientist whose specialty was Alzheimer's disease. This neuroscientist was talking about memory, and I was *listening*, not just because we were there to create a theater piece about the brain, but because of my own crappy memory.

"It's becoming more and more clear that the function of memory is *not* to record the past," he told us, referring to some widely accepted research that showed that the brain creates a new version of a memory every time we recall it. "It's like choosing Save As instead of Save. The memory is changed by whatever happened to influence your perspective since the last time you remembered it. A yellow shirt might be green after several recalls, for instance. So, the memories that we recall the most—a first kiss or some such defining event—are the ones we remember the least accurately."

Several sets of eyes blinked at him from under several furrowed brows.

I ventured, "Well, but then what is memory *for*? I mean, if we don't remember things the way they happened . . ."

"There's no definitive answer, but I have a theory. Would you like to hear it?"

Several heads nodded emphatically.

"I think memory is for storing material from which we can create stories to navigate the *future*."

Several minds were blown.

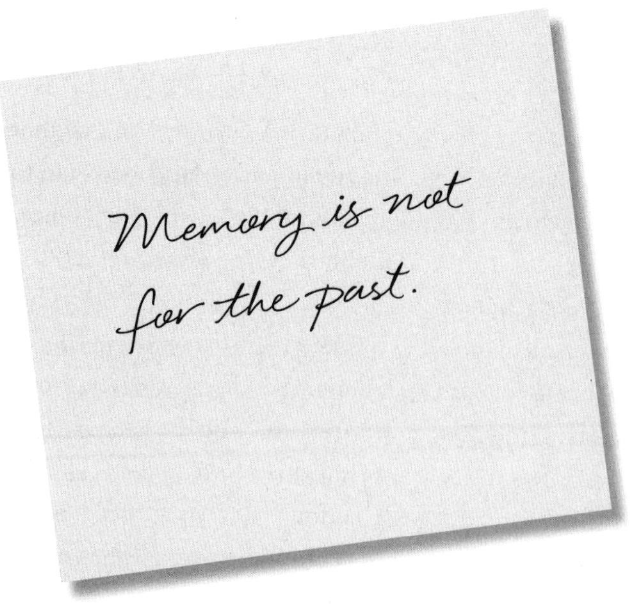
Memory is not
for the past.

Since then, this information about memory has been disseminated in popular media, but at the time of the workshop it was brand new and resulted in identity crises of varying proportions for everyone in that room. As far as we knew, our memories made us who we were. If they weren't accurate, then who were we? So it took a while for me to see the wonderful implications of this theory for writers and artists. Okay, so maybe memory isn't there to define me in some concrete way. But because it's not concrete, it's also not static. It's fluid and ever evolving, and that means . . . it's *limitless.* A limitless resource, right there in my skull! Before, I pictured my memory as a dim attic with some mysterious locked boxes in it. Now, I picture an endless room of endless shelves full of living moments from which I can endlessly create and make meaning.

I no longer worry about whether my memories are accurate or what they mean about me because that's not what memory is for. Memory is for making stuff.

Prompt: Dear Me

I used to be so concerned about my Swiss-cheese memory that I would call family members and old friends and ask them to recount our experiences so I could rebuild them in my head. Once I understood memory better, I thought, *Why not just ask myself?*

Step One: Find yourself. Think of a time in your life you'd like to know more about, or remember more clearly. Locate yourself in that time: How old are you? Where are you living? Are you still living at home? What does your room look like? What is the view outside your window? Let your mind poke around and see what you remember. How did you spend your days and with whom? What were your hobbies? Did you have a favorite

T-shirt? Just close your eyes and see what comes up when you explore this memory.

Step Two: Remember or don't.

1. Write everything you remember about that time of your life: *I was traveling a lot*; *I shouldn't have adopted that cat*; *I had just bought my first piece of real furniture.* Don't worry about whether the memory is authentic or not. Just write as fast as you can for six minutes.
2. Write everything you don't remember about that time of your life: *I don't remember why I was mad at my mom*; *had I gotten the promotion yet or was that later*; *I don't remember how I got by on three hundred dollars a week, who lived next door to me, or what the yard looked like.* Write for six minutes.

Step Three: Reach back.

1. Write a letter that can travel through time to land in the mailbox of the person you were at that time. Write with the intent to communicate with that particular person that you were. Let go of any judgments or romanticizing you may have and get as curious and compassionate as you can.
2. Let him or her know what you've been up to.
3. What would you say about that teacher, your parents, the insomnia, the obsession with so-and-so, the ambition or lack of it?
4. Satisfy your curiosity. Ask your past self to fill in the blanks: *I've been trying to remember . . . Maybe you can help me . . . I'm so curious about . . . I've always wondered why . . .*
5. Sign off with love and respect. Let your past self know that you think of him or her often and with affection. Write for six minutes or more. Then read the letter over. Is it what you wanted to say? Did you ask what you wanted to ask? Make any adjustments to the letter that you feel are necessary.

Step Four: Reach forward. Read what you wrote in step three. Read it with care and interest. Step into your past self's shoes and really take in what your "future" self is saying. Then answer the letter. Write it from the perspective of your past self: *Dear Me, I can't tell you how shocked I was to receive your letter . . .* Write for six minutes or more.

Practice #18: Get Trigger-happy

As of this writing, scientists speculate that our brains have somewhere between 10 terabytes and 2.5 petabytes of "storage." Somehow your brain takes everything that has ever happened to you—huge events, tiny moments, and everything you've felt or sensed or thought or learned, not to mention all the new ideas you're making from connecting the dots between all that stuff every minute of every day—and tucks it all into its folds where it can't ever be lost or stolen. But unlike a computer, you can't just enter a search term into your brain and get a list of relevant hits. Nor is there an effective way to keep a memory from appearing unbidden. This is because instead of search terms your brain uses sensory and emotional cues. For instance, the sight of succotash triggered a visceral childhood memory for me. Hearing Michael Landon's voice might also have triggered the memory, since *Little House on the Prairie* seemed always to be playing in the background during my lima-bean standoffs with my stepfather.

You remember the librarian back when you were a kid and kids went to the library? You'd say, "Do you have a book about ballerinas?" (or "Roman emperors" or "bugs" or "girls who fight crime" or "how to turn onions into hats") and off she'd trot to find you just the right book.

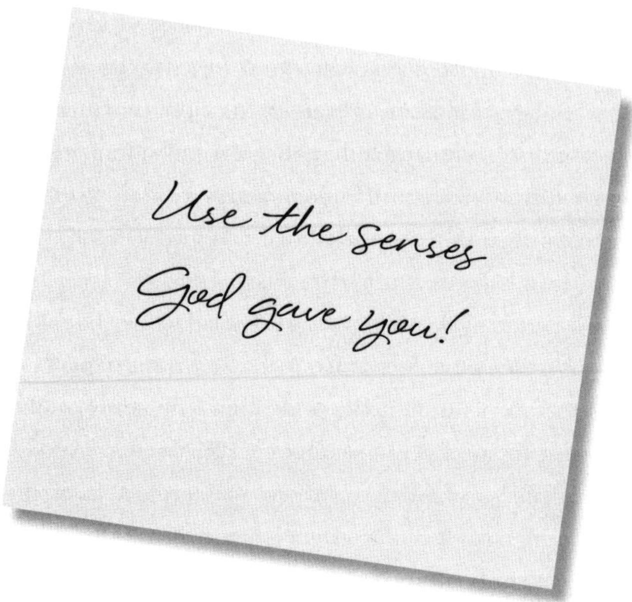
Use the senses
God gave you!

Your senses are a team of five super-librarians. If you give them the right sensory cue, they'll retrieve your childhood camping trips and a job you'd forgotten you had and your mom's hands working the sewing machine. They'll put flavors in your mouth, songs in your ear, and a cold brick of fear in your gut. They have the ability to drop you into any room, tree, or lap you've ever been in, or spook you with a bodily memory of the exact quality of light, texture of fabric, sound of a door slamming, smell of car oil, or flavor of a 50/50 bar.

If you can trigger these memories and feel the emotions and sensations in your body, you can make the reader feel them, too.

Prompt: Put Your Senses to Work

When an actor has to play drunk, he's not actually going to down a fifth of vodka before walking onstage. Actors use sensory recall when they need to realistically convey a physical state they aren't actually experiencing—frostbite, illness, starvation, etc.—or to access and express emotion, as discussed above. What follows are some tools for using your senses to trigger memories of emotions, experiences, and environments to bring depth or specificity to your work—in other words, to help you "make stuff." Your sense of smell is the most powerful of your five "librarians," so we'll start there.

I. Sense of Smell

Step One: Make a list of all the smells you'd take with you to heaven. *Freshly cut lumber*; *baking cookies*; *the back of my child's neck*. No need for descriptions at this point—just list for six minutes.
Step Two: Choose a smell from the list to work with.
Step Three: Put it on the body map. (See p. 223.)
If the smell had a color, what would it be? Grab that crayon.
What areas of your body are affected by the smell? Think about it: a smell doesn't only happen in your nose. It might make your mouth or eyes water, your stomach turn, or your heart beat faster. Use the crayon to identify the affected areas on the body map. Remember there's no way to get this wrong. Whatever it looks or feels like to you is exactly correct.
Step Four: Still working with that chosen smell, answer the following bulleted questions. Remember, memory is fluid, so there is no "correct" answer. Throw the net wide. Make crazy guesses and write things that make no sense. The goal is not to create poetry but to "cross-reference" your senses. By noticing the physical sensations, colors, images, textures, relationships, and experiences associated with the smell, you boost your ability to recall detail. Don't think. Just hold that smell in your nose and move your pen. Spend one to three minutes on each one.

- If the smell had texture, what would it feel like? Fine grit? A thick, soft blanket?

* Where is the smell coming from? Who or what is making the smell?
* What is it doing to you?
* What does it make you want to do?
* Is it associated with a time of year? What season? What weather?
* Is it associated with a time of day? What's the light like? What angle does it come from?
* Is it associated with a place? Where are you most likely to smell it? Indoors or out? What's around you?
* Is it associated with a person or people? Who's around when you smell it? How do you feel about them?
* What does it mean to you? When you smell this smell, what's going to happen?

Step Five: Read through the writing from steps three and four and underline any vivid memories. Underline anything that stirs your emotions or surprises you.

II. Sense of Place

Another way to work with a less-than-photographic memory is to start with just a small scrap and work your way out to the edges, filling in as you go. This uses the cross-referencing abilities of your brain to the fullest, pulling up details you thought were long gone.

Step One: Make a list of rooms you've been in: kitchens, bedrooms, playrooms, classrooms. Include bathrooms, closets, and basements. For example, *Grandma Norton's kitchen*; *the D Street sunroom*; *the violet-papered bedroom*. Don't think. Don't be selective. Just list for six minutes.

Step Two: Choose a room to work with.

Step Three: Write about each of the following for one to three minutes:

* Do you have a favorite spot in that room? Chair, bed, bench, window seat? Find your regular spot and settle in.
* What are you sitting/lying on? How does it receive your weight? Is there give? Texture? Is it smooth, plush, slick, cool, warm?
* What are you wearing? What clothing goes with this room? Shoes? Barefoot?
* What is the light like? Windows? Lamps? Fluorescent?
* What can you hear from this room? Freeway? Voices? Neighbor's TV? Radiator?
* What are the smells in this room? What are the smells coming from beyond this room?
* What's below you, under your feet?
* What's above you?
* Someone enters the room and speaks to you. Where do you feel their voice in your body? What does their voice do to you?

Step Four: Write for six minutes about something that happened (or didn't happen) to you in that room.

Step Five: Read back through the writing from step three and underline any evocative words, phrases, or details—as in those that evoke a response. Notice your responses.

Bonus Prompts: No Sense Left Untriggered

* List sounds that you heard every day as a child and what they meant. Then list sounds that your characters would hear every day.
* Also try "My Mother's/Father's Cooking," "Places I Can Never Go Again," and "Injuries I've Received" to get at memories through your senses.

11

Truth—Fear of Lying

Lay Down the First Layer / Dig into Change

When I first moved to the small town of Ojai, in California, I lived in a commune for a while. Since I planned to return to New York as soon as I'd finished a draft of my play, I was excited to find this place. They charged little rent, offsetting the cost with chores, cooking, and gardening assignments, and all the basic living necessities were provided. I sublet my Brooklyn apartment to my ex, grabbed a towel, a toothbrush, and my computer, and that was that.

The commune had mandatory weekly councils. For non–First Nations peoples, a council is basically a meeting made much more onerous by the employment of ostensibly Native American ritual. We sat on the floor around some burning incense and passed the talking stick, twenty or so hippies and me. The purpose of the council was to bring up glitches in the community system and discuss fixes. Usually it was stuff like *Could we pull together a crew to put in the tomato seedlings?* or *Could those who cook be more vigilant about hidden meat products when preparing communal meals?*

But, invariably, someone would close their eyes upon receiving the talking stick and take a few deliberate, long, "cleansing" breaths.

When that happened, I knew they were going to begin with, "I have to speak my truth . . ."

The first few times, I thought, "Oh, wow, their *truth*. Something important is happening," because when the holder of the talking stick said "my truth" there was usually an air of the sacred about it, as though their truth was a shamanistic sacrifice earned through a three-day peyote ritual or something.

But I soon came to understand that with this phrase we were ritually sanctioning a venting of personal grievance directly onto someone in the circle, e.g., "If Maya is going to overeat, she should pay for a larger food share. I have continually found the almond butter jar empty, and I don't feel she should have three helpings of dessert."

And I would think, *Why not just whack her with the talking stick? That would be less horrible.*

Though I didn't like this part of the weekly councils, I couldn't dismiss it, either. I had the opposite issue, in that I couldn't get my truth out. The more truthful it was, the less able I was to say it aloud—or write it. So who was I to dismiss some ruthless truthiness? Maybe I wasn't truthy enough.

Practice #19: Lay Down the First Layer

I have often heard it said that "the secret to good writing is the successful communication of the truth."

Oh, great. No pressure, right? This is the kind of statement that gives my creative spirit the shrivels.

First off, what *is* the truth? Look up *true* in any dictionary and you'll find somewhere between fifteen and twenty-five meanings for the word. Is it true if it can be proven, as in *true to life*? Is it true if it's painful to say, as in *true confessions*? If it risks upsetting someone, as in *the truth hurts*? If it reveals or declares the authentic self, as in *to thine own self be true*? And what makes the truth worth sharing? If it evokes an emotional reaction? If it's shocking? If it's extraordinary in scope? If it's exotic or inspiring or raw or gritty or deeply felt?

Someone once gave me some great advice—and I wish I could remember who it was—about how to behave in a meeting or a group discussion: when you're hit with an urgent bolt of insight and it feels like it must be shared right this minute, because the truth just became so *clear*—that's the time to stay silent. Wait until the urgency passes, and if it still feels true, *then* say it. I've found this is very hard to do, but most of the time, when the emotion dissipates, my big, important, insightful truth needs some unpacking. This a good example of what I call "first-layer truth."

First-layer truth is driven by strong emotion, by feelings that want *out. Now.* The pen is fueled by a hot desire for acknowledgment, relief, solutions, and maybe just a smidge of revenge. Great. Get that on the page. The emotional pressure behind it is like the nitro that blasts open an entrance to the next layer, where more complexity will begin to emerge.

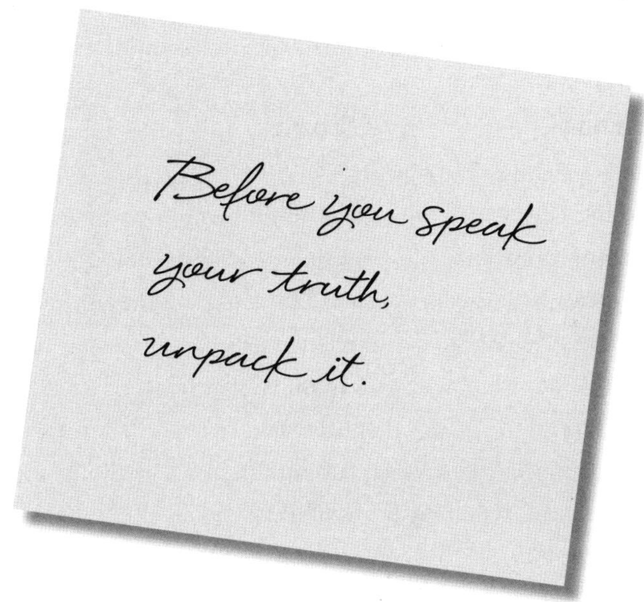
Before you speak
your truth,
unpack it.

First-layer truth takes a variety of forms:

Truth as a stick. In this form of FLT (First-layer Truth), there are good guys and bad guys, and the truth aims to expose who was right and who was wrong, presenting the proof as if in a court of law. There are blameless victims and contemptible villains and the world shall know the truth of it all. If your story is about how Aunt Charlotte ruined your life, you're probably hanging out in the first layer.

Truth as confession. Maybe it's because he was raised Catholic, but my husband is a compulsive confessor. It's a wonderful quality in a spouse, really. When I come home from a week away the house may be pristine, but I have only to ask him and he'll tell me how he pulled the dining room table in front of the sofa and made a junk food island from which he watched anime for three days straight. He simply can't help telling on himself, like he's spring-loaded for it. I see a lot of confessional writing these days, blurty TMI that blushes and squirms onto the page. It's driven sometimes by the thrill of exposure, sometimes by the hope of more page views, sometimes by the need for relief or absolution or to not be alone with it any longer, and sometimes by all of the above.

Truth as fact. This form of FLT isn't always accompanied by strong emotion. It emerges more from the need to honor the past by documenting it with scrupulous adherence to the facts.

Truth as a soapbox. This writing seeks to relay a message or teach a lesson. It scrabbles for the moral high ground. It speaks truth to power and it openly aims to change hearts and minds.

Truth as triumph. This story details the author's dauntless overcoming of bullies and detractors, impossible odds, or the forces of nature. It's a heart-pounding true-life account of staring down death, enduring suffering, kicking ass and taking names. It's muscular and adrenalized and often neglects to mention the vulnerable aspects of the self that are wounded or even sacrificed in the undertaking of such difficulties.

Truth as authenticity. This writing harbors a sense that there is a sacred, authentic truth that can be discovered and expressed. This can set up a yearning akin to that of a prospector hoping for that big shiny nugget of gold to appear in his pan. For me, the yearning to release this authentic self through writing motivated a great deal of first-layer stuff before I realized that my authentic self is ever changing.

The great thing about first layers is that they lead to deeper layers, and for that we love them. Strap yourself to the heat-seeking missile of first-layer truth. Don't fear it. Ride the emotional momentum of it and fill page after page with vindication, confession, vitriol, aggrandizement, navel-gazing, finger-wagging, and obsessive documentation. Indulge the drive fully, wherever it springs from, without self-consciousness or self-reproach, knowing that there is no better mining tool for this stage of the work.

Once you've blasted through the crust, you can begin to shift your intention toward discovering a more complex and, yes, layered truth. The truthful writing I'm talking about doesn't strive to prove, teach, or document anything about you. It strives to reveal something to you and through you. Yes, first *to* you. *Then* through you.

All writers have heard the maxim "Write what you know." But I believe it will go so much better for you if you write toward the next thing you're *trying* to know.

Even when the story is made strictly of real-life events and facts, there will be something to discover in the process of unlayering it. Stories and art, even when they are representational and factual, are designed to reveal more truth than the facts alone can convey.

I want to be clear: I'm not saying there is an authentic truth that you must strive to express through your work. The word "authentic" suggests something fixed and verifiable, yet the so-called authentic self changes minute by minute, provoked and pressured by obstacles, conflict, natural forces, and biology. Every microexperience, from hearing a new song to drinking coffee, pushes me to change. If my authentic self is ever evolving, so is my authentic truth. I can write about the same experience at five-year intervals and it will be a different story—with a differently nuanced truth—because I will be a different person every time I write it.

The truth is something you meet and unfold through the work, layer by layer. You'll know it when you've hit it because it will feel like the answer you didn't know the question for. You discover it when you see how your life experiences, when processed and presented in a certain way, reveal something about you that, in turn, reveals something about how we humans face life's challenges.

And if your Aunt Charlotte is still bent out of shape about how you portrayed her after you dig through the layers, I refer you to this Anne Lamott quote: "If people wanted you to write warmly about them, they should have behaved better."

Prompt: One Stick, Many Uses

The full indulgence of first-layer, emotional truth can be very freeing. Or, if you're somewhat reserved in nature, it might feel utterly mortifying. Either way, I encourage you to really lean in to the following exercises and be shrill, intolerant, victim-y, or any number of things you find it impossible to be in real life. I encourage you to let go of whether the writing is "appropriate" and go for a sense of release.

Step One: Whack others. Write a tell-all, no-holds-barred, somebody-done-me-wrong story about the ex, coworker, boss, frenemy, or neighbor who bullied, betrayed, or belittled you. Show them at their full asshat worst. Pour the injustice and the way you truly felt about it right onto the page with no tempering or processing whatsoever. Present the facts and seek justice. Write for six minutes or more.

Step Two: Whack yourself. Confess a story of blowing it, failing, falling flat, getting it wrong, making a fool of yourself. Find that moment when you were in your absolute loser glory and just romp around in there like a Labrador in a mud puddle. Get it all down: the misconduct, the mistakes, the humiliation. Write for six minutes or for as long as you can stand it.

Step Three: Dig, stir, stoke, poke, and deconstruct—the truth remix.

1. Rewrite either your step one or step two work from another character's point of view—this could be an innocent bystander or the asshat himself. Do your best to fully inhabit this point of view, considering the temperament, traits, and motives of the character you've chosen. Write in the first person, include their inner monologue, and tell their version. What part do they play in the drama? Do they have a vested interest in the conflict? Don't plan or try to be interesting. Just stoke your curiosity and jump in. Write for six minutes.
2. Rewrite either story from a third-person omniscient point of view. In this telling, there is a narrator who can see into the minds of all the characters, so we get to hear the thoughts and feel the feelings of all involved. Don't worry about good writing. Just commit to the task. Write fast. Write badly. Do this for six minutes or more.
3. Rewrite the story as a fairy tale, with kings, witches, castles, magical objects, fools, and enchanted creatures. Write yourself as a fairy-tale protagonist—princess, orphan, wizard, warrior, whatever feels right. Don't plan. Don't worry about a one-to-one translation of the real events and characters into their fairy-tale counterparts. Just launch from "Once upon a time . . ." and be curious to see what comes out of your pen. Write for six minutes or more.

Step Four: Read your exercises over and underline anything, no matter how small, that feels like new information.

Practice #20: Dig into Change

If it's hard to locate the truly authentic self because we're always changing, then perhaps change *is* what's true. Everything is in flux. Even granite is being continuously transformed, however slowly, by lichen and weather and tree roots and microorganisms.

Change is the closest thing I've found to a universal truth. It's our only real constant. Strive as we might for stability, something is always coming along to shake it up—illness, insight, financial crashes, acts of God, pregnancy, policy shifts, breakups, death, or just plain old outgrowing things.

You've probably noticed that most stories start with a life disruption for the protagonist, whose "normal" is shattered by a knock at the door, an act of violence, a juicy opportunity, or a meteor screaming toward Earth. Yanked out of her known world, our protagonist comes up against her limits, taps deeper inner resources than she knew were available to her, and ultimately embraces transformation and triumphs.

Change is creation
in action.

Or, in a tragedy, she successfully avoids all that and scrambles back to the safety of her "normal." Our most beloved stories explore the nature of change—not of changing others or changing the world, but of the characters themselves having to change, to grow.

There is no ground more common or truth more shared than change, which is why we need stories and art to explore the nature of change and prepare us to tangle with it. Change tests us, exposes what's not working, and opens us to new understanding. It's where our wisdom is earned and our values are formed, and that's about as close to an authentic truth as we get. Change is creation in action, so it's a great place for us to create from.

Prompt: Mine Change for Truth

Step One: Finish the sentence "I used to . . ." or "I no longer . . ." *I used to drink Diet Coke. I used to be Lutheran. I no longer have my coin collection.* Finish it as many different ways as you can in six minutes.
Step Two: Choose something from step one that draws you in. It can be big or small, but it should represent an overcoming, something you're on the other side of.
Step Three: Answer each of the following questions as they apply to the overcoming you've chosen. Don't get thinky or analytical, and don't try to get to the bottom of anything. Just let the questions stir up your curiosity, set the timer, and write your way toward an answer. Give each question at least two minutes.

* What external forces, people, or events caused you to change?
* Did you want to change? Explain.
* What belief, value system, or aspect of self did you have to leave behind in order to change?

- What value was gained as a result of the change?
- Who would you be today if the change hadn't occurred?

Bonus Prompts: More Ways to Mine Change

Make a list entitled "Beginnings" and write down a business you started, a first date, a birth, an inkling, a consciousness shift, a new lease. List all the beginnings you can think of for six minutes.

Make a list entitled "Endings" and write down graduations, breakups, a letting go, a loss. List all the endings you can think of for six minutes. Notice when things show up on both the "Beginnings" and "Endings" lists.

The "Mine Change" prompt can be applied to fictional protagonists to investigate their internal struggles. Have your character do the exercise just like you did it, but let them use your hand and pen.

Study change in books and movies. Notice what the character must confront internally. Is there some belief or fear holding her back from solving the problems she's facing? What does it take to make her see it, and how does she become willing to change?

12

Dark Matter—Fear of Whining

Be the Shaman, Not the Shame / Make Your Medicine

A common worry among the writers I've worked with about their writing is, "It's too dark. It's too depressing. It's TMI. Nobody will want to read this." I've found it a very difficult concern to alleviate, which is not surprising, since I, like most people, was taught that complaining and whining are big social sins and I shouldn't burden others with my problems, much less write about them. Then I came across this tiny little myth that explained it better than any fifty-page treatise I could have written on the subject. Like so many myths, it's pretty hair-raising, so brace yourself. Ready? Here we go:

In an Inuit village, a long time ago, the old shaman died. When he'd breathed his last breath, the good spirits swept through the village searching for the young person who would be trained to fill his role. They chose an adolescent boy and took him down, down, down, into the underworld. There they cut him up into pieces so that no two bones touched each other.

I know—gruesome, right? But wait, it gets worse.

Then the good spirits called to the evil spirits, who came and gnawed all the flesh off the young man's dismembered bones. When the future shaman was completely gnawed bare and not one of his bones touched another, the good spirits shooed out the bad spirits. As the demons left, now sluggish, slow, and fat from feasting, the good spirits scrupulously recorded the name of each one.

Then they put all the bones back together, re-membering the boy, being very careful since the new shaman would forever feel the missing piece if any bone was mislaid. They then drummed and sang new flesh onto his bones.

But before he was welcomed into the village as the new shaman, there was one last thing to do. The good spirits presented him with the record they'd kept of all the bad spirits that had gnawed on his bones, since the new shaman only had the power to cure the illnesses caused by those demons; he was unable to cure any illness caused by an evil demon that had not been present at his dismemberment.

Practice #21: Be the Shaman, Not the Shame

There is no way to get through life without some pain. There are bad spirits, bad people, and bad breaks that will get their teeth far enough into you to leave marks on the bone. When is it appropriate to tap life's pain and share it in your art? This question can be such a trap: either you fear burdening someone else's soul with your trials, or worse, you fear your trials are *nothing* compared to those of people with *real* problems.

This is a Catch-22 woven strictly of shame. Why there is so much shame around pain and suffering is a matter best left to the anthropologists and psychologists, but one thing's for certain: shame is the squeakiest wheel in the Inner Critic Killjoy Club. "You're going to look weak, you're betraying the family code of silence, nobody likes a Debbie Downer, turn that frown upside down, what makes you think your problems are so special, stop whining and go help someone who has real problems." *Squeak* effing *squeak*, *squeak*, *squeak*!

While it can seem like these mean thoughts are your own, I guarantee they originate from an external source. There are some pernicious ideas about pain and suffering going around, and they are handed out to us good and early in life. Here are just a few:

* Stoic equals heroic. Ignore your pain.
* Pain is punishment. You did something wrong.
* Pain is inconvenient. Medicate that shit.
* Pain means you're special. Wear it like a badge.
* Pain requires action. Pay it back or pay it forward.

Try this one instead: Pain is information. Whether physical or emotional, pain tells you something needs to change or that something is changing. For instance: you touch a hot stove. Ouch! The pain makes you look at the stove. *What is it about that stove? Aha! That stove is hot. I need to change how I work with it. Next time I'll use an oven mitt.*

Or how about when you burst into tears in a pitch meeting? That sucks, right? Your instinct might be to pretend that it never happened, buck up, batten down, and be tougher. But that's a waste of some perfectly good information. Pain is telling you to look at something: you never cried when pitching before. What's changed? What needs to change? If you don't look, the pain will keep trying to get your attention.

There's a reason they call them growing pains. Soreness is a well-known symptom of a muscle growing stronger. Pain, physical or emotional, is not the whole story, but it tells you where to look for what grew or is growing or is in need of growth, and *that* is the story. When we tap our pain for the creative process, we are inviting the wisdom of growth and change to reveal itself, and this is a good thing.

Pain is a symptom
of growth.

Prompt: The List of Bad Spirits

Step One: Make a list of all the "bad spirits" that ate away at you. These might be people, places, organizations, jobs, addictions, illnesses—anything that left a mark. Don't worry about its literary or therapeutic value at this point. Don't worry about being fair or taking responsibility. Just list anything that got its teeth into you and caused you pain. List for six minutes. (Save this list for use in the next prompt.)

Step Two: Make a list of any "good spirits" that were key in putting you back together after you were taken apart. This might be friends, family members, therapists, teachers, mentors, a song or poem or story, a workshop. List for six minutes.

Did anything appear on both lists? It's important to remember that some forces can be both destructive and healing.

Practice #22: Make Your Medicine

While our achievements and successes can uplift and inspire others, it's our suffering that invites connection. Everyone suffers, strive as we might to avoid it, because suffering is a symptom of change and, as we've discussed, change is the one constant in life that unites us.

Think of the stories that saved you, saved your relationships, lifted you up, and gave you the perspective you needed to keep going. These stories were written by people willing to mill their own dark experiences in order to remind you that you are not alone.

How do I live with this guilt/sorrow/anger? How do I see a door when all I've been shown are walls? Where do I find the courage or the faith to love again? How do I put myself back together when I've been blown apart by loss? These questions can best be answered by art, songs, stories, and poetry.

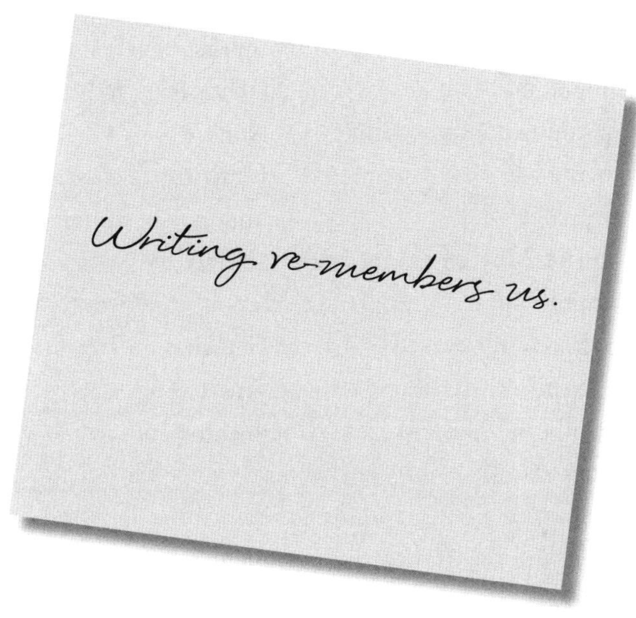

So really, what we share when we create from these life difficulties is not simply the painful dismemberment, but our intimate and bone-deep knowledge about life. Transformative and powerful re-membering is what allows us to do this, because through that process we are sanctified to speak to and heal others who have been injured by these same difficulties. Sometimes this re-membering is done with the help of a counselor or mentor or loved one. More often than not, it's the creative process that re-members us, because when we create from our experiences, we're bound to understand something new about them.

But even the creative process has its "good spirits." While we stereotypically think of the artist as isolated in her process, this is rarely the way it works. We don't do it alone. There are teachers, mentors, developmental editors, critique partners, first readers, analysts, and the other artists we admire who play the oh-so-critical good-spirit role as we take our experiences apart and re-member them into art.

We're healed by the art of others, we heal ourselves in the process of making art, and that art, in turn, has the power to heal. Yeah, art is some seriously good medicine.

Knowledge, like how to start a fire or program a computer, can be delivered in a number of ways, but meaning is best shared through art and stories. Meaning as in, *What does it all mean?* This is what a story addresses. Stories and art are how we understand our world, how we understand ourselves, how we make ourselves understood, and how we break through to new understanding.

But stories that gloss over the pain of life do not instruct or heal. Neither do stories that simply express raw, unprocessed pain. Think of this like having a really bad flu: for days you're in a twilight place between life and death, but you squeak through. You live. In the process of fighting off the virus, your body creates antibodies. Those antibodies not only protect you from being reinfected, but they can be used to create medicine that will help others. This is what we want to express and preserve—the medicine, not the virus itself.

By writing about the people and situations that took you down, ate away at you, and gnawed your bones, you make medicine. Like the shaman, you have the power to heal those wounds in others because you have healed those wounds in yourself.

At its best, a story says, *No matter how thoroughly and violently life takes you apart, you can be put back together. It's the hard work of being human, but it's possible, and when it's done, you'll be more than you were before.* Even in a tragic story, we see what happens when humans aren't put back together with care, and that's good medicine, too.

Prompt: Distill Your Medicine

Step One: Read back through your list of things that ate away at you from step one of the previous prompt. Circle or underline an item from the list. This can be anything that has some energy to it or makes you curious, but please choose something that you've had time to heal from. Write the name of that "bad spirit" at the top of the next blank space.

Step Two: Look at your body map (see p. 223) and mark the places the bad spirit did the most damage with its teeth, claws, and venom. Maybe it went after your heart. Did it make it hard for you to breathe? Did it make your stomach hurt? Did it give you bad dreams or hallucinations? Maybe it was an actual physical injury or illness. What did it feel like? Let yourself gravitate to a color and draw the injuries on the body map wherever you felt them literally, emotionally, or figuratively.

Step Three: Working with that same bad spirit, jump back to your notebook and, letting your body map inspire you, name the demon's most dangerous qualities. Give yourself permission to leave the literal person, place, or thing behind, regarding it as just a point of departure. Let yourself imagine it in its bad-spirit form. What qualities and powers does it use to take you apart? Does it have razor-sharp nails to shred your will? Limbs that extend and retract so it can reach you no matter where you try to hide? A jaw that unhinges to swallow you whole? The ability to appear small and helpless in order to lure you in? Just list anything that comes through about its nature, appearance, abilities, habits, or effects. Write for six minutes.

Step Four: If you haven't already, write down the spirit's demon name: Disappearing Ink Demon or Refrigerator Hag or Sapsucking Spirit. If you don't know its name, feel free to guess or make something up or leave it and come back to it later.

Step Five: Return to the body map and draw the powers that you gained when you were put back together after this bad spirit took you apart. Did you develop extra-sensitive hearing? The ability to read people quickly? Did you take up martial arts, become sensitive to beauty, study massage and find that you could locate and relieve other people's pain? Don't think, just pick up a crayon and start drawing whatever that looks like to you.

Step Six: Write the step-by-step instructions for how to fight, neutralize, or cast out this demon/bad spirit. For instance:

* Gather your supplies: No less than fifty feet of rope, a forked stick, a mirror, and an upside-down rowboat.
* Prop up one end of the rowboat with the forked end of the stick and tie the end of the rope to the bottom of the stick.
* Place the mirror under the boat. This demon can't resist a mirror.
* Take the other end of the rope and hide behind a rock, etc.

Bonus Prompts: Other Distillation Methods

* Write three lists (three minutes each):
  1. "Stories I Always Tell"
  2. "Stories My Family Always Tells"
  3. "Stories I Never Tell"
* Read back through the three lists and choose a story to work with. Write the full story in thirty minutes.
* Write it again in ten minutes.
* Now write the story in ten minutes again using only one-syllable words.

13

The Unknown—Looking for Proof

Don't Wait until You Are Ready / Plight Your Troth

There's a picture of me at age five, one of those old Kodak snapshots with the trim white border and washed-out colors, and in it, I'm dressed as a bride, standing in front of a white picket fence. It's Halloween, and this is the costume my mother has made for me, complete with a ribboned bouquet. Under the smart pillbox hat with its neat little veil I wear a grim smile. I had wanted to be a fairy or a witch—something magic. Something that flies.

I didn't have a problem with brides, I just never wanted to be one—even at age five.

In my midthirties I fell in love with Chris. Right after we got together, several of our friends initiated divorces, which looked to me like the equivalent of dropping napalm on your life. I told Chris I had always thought marriage was a good way to ruin a great relationship, and was relieved when he agreed.

But three years in, he changed his tune. Maybe I should have been moved that he loved me enough to court total devastation, but I wasn't.

"Why borrow trouble?" I said. "The only way we'll ever get divorced is if we get married. No." Best, I thought, to shut this down as quickly as possible. "No, no, absolutely no."

We went back and forth for months, and it became clear that it really meant something to him. I couldn't just brush him and his wide-open heart aside.

I grilled all my girlfriends, hoping to hear something that would settle the matter—in my favor, of course. Married, divorced, or remarried, they all urged me to go for it. Judy was a few years into her marriage, and it looked like it was going well. I pressed her on the divorce thing.

"It's a Catch-22, kind of. You're scared because it means everything, but, like, too bad, because you don't get to know how it turns out. But anyway, I don't think it's about some goal of succeeding. I think it's about becoming more than the sum of just your own parts, you know?"

"Why can't we just do that without getting married?"

"All I know is something . . . *shifts*. When you say 'I do'? It's alchemical."

"Until you get divorced."

Judy raised an eyebrow. "What do you think, Deb—you're never going to have problems if you don't get married?"

". . . Maybe."

I didn't like to think of myself as playing it safe, but Judy shined a light on the piece of my heart that I was hiding. Marriage was full-frontal exposure: it brought your community out to witness the whole naked launch of your combined ship into the waters of the unknown. There was no map or set of instructions that would ensure success. There were no money-back guarantees.

Our wedding was the best day of my life, and the scariest. But Judy was right: something did shift when we said our vows. Chris said it felt like metal melting and fusing. For me, it felt like being folded into something big and powerful: we became greater than the sum of our parts.

Practice #23: Don't Wait until You Are Ready

You receive the "proposal" in the form of an impulse, a vision, an idea, a pressure in your chest that can only be relieved by movement of the pen, the brush, the body, the strings, or the keys. But soon an ugly little feeling surfaces like a bubble in an oil slick, demanding assurances: "Where is this going? What is the plan? What is the probability of success?"

Writers might attend conferences for years, hoping to find that magic secret to success. Maybe they rewrite the first three chapters over and over, not moving on until an agent or editor pronounces the story marketable. Maybe they aren't going to write a single word until they know exactly where the story ends. These are some of the myriad ways writers delay committing to a story.

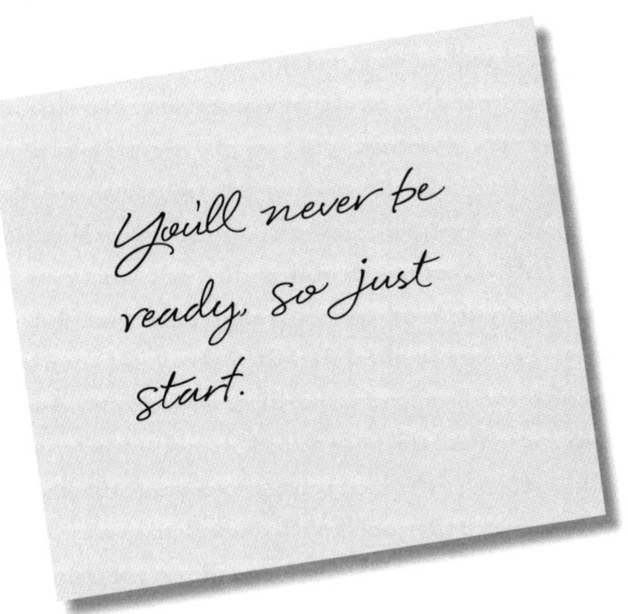

You'll never be
ready, so just
start.

"But hey," you might say, "we wouldn't go on a road trip without a destination, without knowing if the trip will take two weeks or two years. That wouldn't even be safe." Here's how creation is different from a road trip: the destination emerges *after* you've embarked upon the journey.

And anyway, what's so great about being "safe"? Does that even exist? The more information, the more laws, systems, weapons, and good nutrition we have, the more we accept safety as a promise. We live in a time where people are outraged by the unexpected and insured against acts of God. But when we cross the threshold into the creative world, this mentality works against us. In the creative realm, we don't want to increase our security, we want to increase our tolerance for risk.

I want to be clear, I'm not talking about risking your neck or your life savings. I'm not saying get a tattoo, quit your job, and move to an artists co-op in order to show your true commitment. It's not about risking your security or stability. It's about risking your heart.

Looking at the blank page can feel like a life-and-death proposition. You will die of heartbreak if you don't write. You will die of terror if you do. It's how, I imagine, people feel when contemplating parenthood. But would anyone ever have children if they waited until they felt emotionally or mentally ready?

The good news: the more time you spend in the creative realm, the more comfortable you become with not knowing what to expect. You become more adept at reading the landscape and noting the subtle shifts in weather and so you become more curious, too.

So just start. From wherever you are, with whatever you have. Write that first horrible, shapeless draft as fast as you can. You don't know what it's going to become, so just launch and move with serious commitment in its general direction. Dream, push, drive, finger-paint, and barf it onto the page as if moving your pen is what keeps your heart beating, is what keeps *everyone's* heart beating. Make your writing that important. Say "I do." Say "I am." Say "we are" and commit to finding out what that means as you go along.

Prompt: Hopes and Fears

Step One: Risk Assessment. Make a list with two columns. In the left column, list all the bad things that could happen if you throw caution to the wind and commit to your writing; in the right column, list the good things that could happen. For example:

Bad things that could happen	Good things that could happen
Rejection	Acceptance
I won't finish	Lift the pressure on my heart caused by holding the story in
It won't be as good as I want it to be	Discovery
People might laugh	People might laugh

Practice #24: Plight Your Troth

I used to think that faith was the same thing as knowing. *This love is forever, the universe will provide, I'm on the right track* . . . If my faith was strong enough, it became true.

In marriage, though, there is no *knowing*, and no amount of faith will change that. I don't get to know how long this person will stay with me, whether he will change drastically, whether that change will bring us closer or take him in a direction where I can't follow. This is both the most uncomfortable thing about marriage and the most ennobling. In a "knowing" scenario, I am either constantly searching for proof of my beliefs or I'm resting assured that my beliefs are correct. In a "not knowing" scenario, I'm showing up to the unfolding truth, awake and alive to the mystery as it's revealed in its own good time. In this latter way of being married, commitment is a loving place in which to practice my risk tolerance.

These days, I think of faith as a way to respect and engage with the mystery.

I avoided marriage because I didn't want to make a promise that big if I couldn't be assured of keeping it. I thought of the marital contract as a binding assurance of no-matter-whatness. I pledge. I promise. I plight thee my troth.

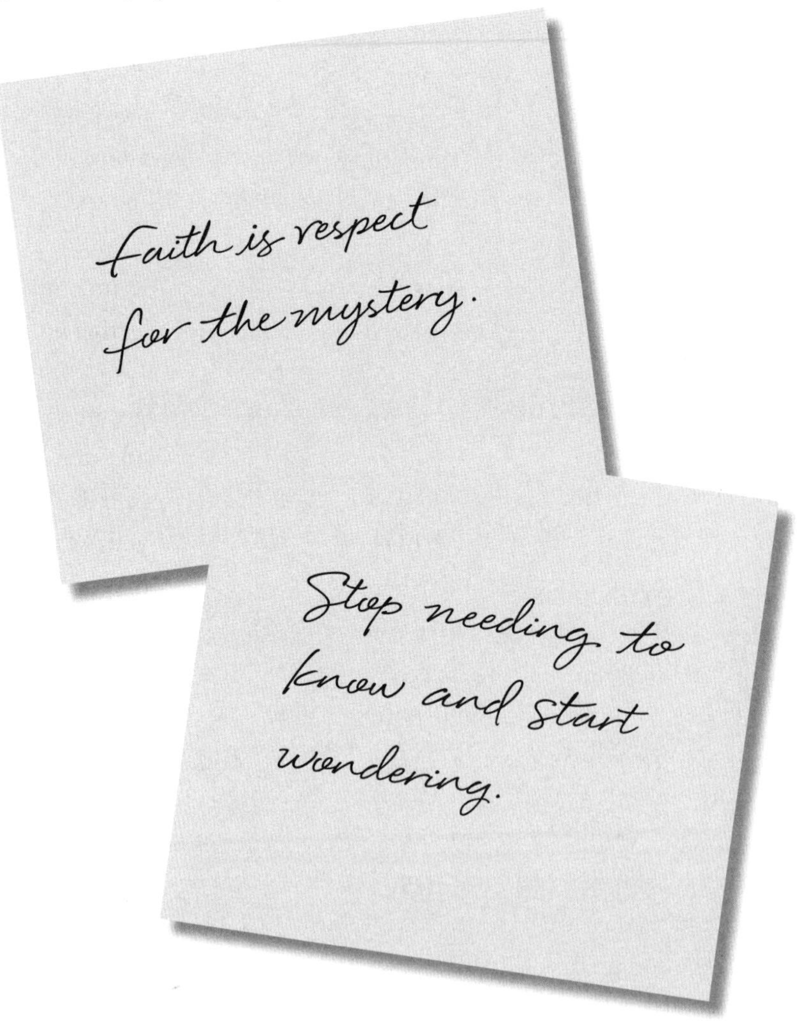

Faith is respect for the mystery.
Stop needing to know and start wondering.

Did you know that the derivation of the word *plight* is a combination of danger, risk, wrinkle, and obligation? And *troth* means truth. I plight my troth. I risk my truth. I give up sole control. I understand that there will be wrinkles. I endanger my "known."

Marriage was much more robust when I stopped needing to know and started wondering. I wonder what he's wrestling with right now? I wonder why we're fighting about this? I wonder what will happen? Who are we becoming? Where is this taking us?

To create is to make something new. Because it's never existed before, we can't know everything about it until it's fully here. We don't engage with the writing process to show or prove what we know but to transcend the limitations of what we know—to move toward the next thing we're trying to know. This means spending time in that uninsurable, liminal space of the *Un*known, where the really interesting stuff happens. You're not alone in the unknown. Your creation will meet you there in good faith, and together you'll both become something more.

You don't get to be good at marriage before you get married, and you can't know what treasures lie on the other side of a creative doorway until you're well through it. Let yourself feel the crazed mix of hope and fear this evokes, then sweep your writing up in your arms and carry it across the threshold. Invest everything and the writing will give you something *new*, something you couldn't possibly have discovered by waiting, planning, or trying to figure it out. And at that point, you will have become bigger than the sum of your parts.

Prompt: Known Unknowns

Step One: Launch from the sentence starter "I know . . ." and finish it as many different ways as you can. *I know my name is Deb*; *I* *know I'm writing this sentence; I know trees grow up toward the sky.* Write for six minutes.

Step Two: Launch from the sentence starter "I wonder . . ." and finish it as many different ways as you can. *I wonder what my lizard does while I'm at work; I wonder who they'll elect to chair the committee; I wonder why my mom won't talk about her childhood.* Write for six minutes.

Step Three: Read through each list and notice which one makes you feel more like writing.

Step Four: Read through the writing from step two and underline anything that draws you in, piques your interest, or feels like an invitation.

Step Five: Choose one of your underlined items and accept the invitation. Let it be the starting place for an energetic exploration.

Bonus Prompt: Known Unknowns for Character Development

Have any of your characters do steps one and two of the above prompt. Just give them control of your pen and have them finish the sentence starters "I know . . ." and "I wonder . . ."

14

Voice—What Is It and How Do I Get One?

Discover Your Limitations

In acting school, I learned that 1) most people don't use the full capacity and range of their voices and 2) most people don't know what they actually sound like.

I spent three years rolling on the floor, warbling, bleating, buzzing like a band saw, looking into my mouth with a hand mirror, pretending my head was a train on tracks or a balloon on a string. I breathed into my intercostals. I breathed out of the top of my skull. I even flopped over at the waist and breathed through my anus; theater is not for the squeamish.

Early on, Gerald, the first-year voice teacher, vise-gripped my ribs and commanded me to push his weirdly strong hands apart with my breath. I needed to replace the air he'd squeezed out of me or faint, so I sucked in and felt, one by one, every separate muscle and the vastly complex array of actions responsible for bringing breath into my body, and I was forever changed. I was encased in a somatic musical instrument, I realized, and I hadn't even begun to discover its potential.

One of my classmates, Sarah, was both beautiful and talented, but she had a sharp, nasal voice. Gerald plied her with technique, assuring her that increasing her vocal range would increase the variety of parts she could play.

"What about Lucille Ball? What about Jennifer Tilly? I mean, do we all have to sound like Meryl Streep?" she challenged.

"We don't want you to sound like anyone but you, darling," Gerald would say. "It's range we're after."

It was a compelling question—should we all be going for a pleasantly modulated tone with a round, jammy resonance? What about Fran Drescher? She rode her exaggerated nasality to megastardom on *The Nanny*. Couldn't Sarah make a career as an actor despite her voice—or maybe even because of it? Would expanding or modulating her vocal capacity and range eradicate something mysteriously, essentially *her*?

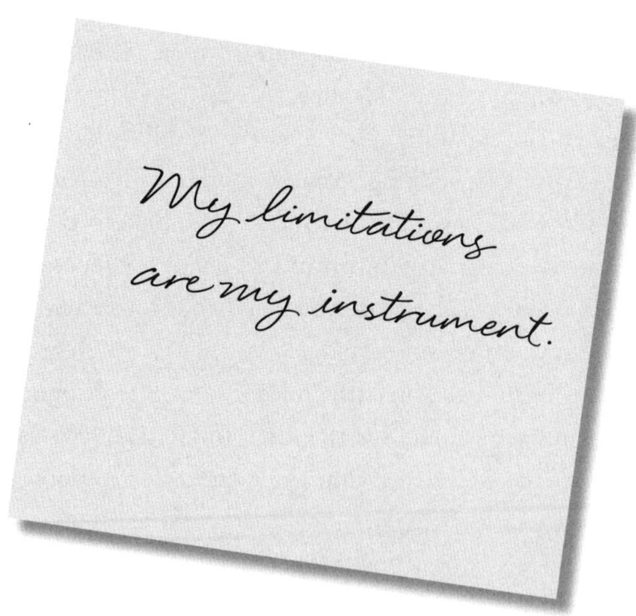
My limitations
are my instrument.

Practice #25: Discover Your Limitations

Voice, voice, voice. You have to find your voice—that's what all the writing books say. Well, okay, but where do you look for it? How do you know when you've found it? How do you develop it? It's like getting to the critical moment in the kitchen and finding that the recipe says, "Now imbue the mixture with delicious flavor." What makes a voice delicious? What if my voice is salty when everyone's in the market for sweet?

In vocal technique class they called it "learning to use your instrument." But I can see now that what I was actually learning was to use my *limitations*. My body was basically a big wind instrument through which I pushed air in order to make a sound—and what is a wind instrument if not a series of carefully crafted limitations that can be controlled to make music? The enclosed space of my noggin was a resonating chamber. My torso was a bellows. The bones of my nasal cavity and the surface of my hard palate were amplifiers. My throat muscles, lips, and tongue were the keys that changed the tone and pitch.

It's the specific and unrepeatable limitations provided by the size and shape of these enclosed spaces and surfaces that give my voice its distinct sound. When you hear a trumpet, there's no mistaking it for a flute. Moreover, you can also tell whether it's Louis Armstrong or Miles Davis playing that trumpet. Both artists were extremely proficient technically, but each used technique to free his own signature sound. It's the same for writers. We hone our technique so that we can develop and expand and explore our own unique voice.

For writers, voice can be broken into two areas of development: learning technique and learning your instrument. Learning technique (also called "craft" or "style") involves things like parts of speech, story structure, point of view, showing versus telling, rewriting, and an endless amount of stuff, really. We're not concerned with technique here: I'm all about helping you learn your instrument.

Whereas the actor's instrument is her body, the writer's instrument is her perspective. Your perspective is a product of the limitations imposed by genetics, environment, experience, senses, brain chemistry, and your particular "spark." You breathe the world in, and it resonates against the very specific limitations of your perspective to create your one and only voice.

Some wise person, possibly Allen Ginsberg, said, "Notice what you notice." That is a creative person's M.O. But to explore and strengthen your voice, you must also notice *how* you notice. Until I became aware of all the autonomic processes that were involved in creating my voice, I couldn't do a lot with it. Awareness is the first step to mastery.

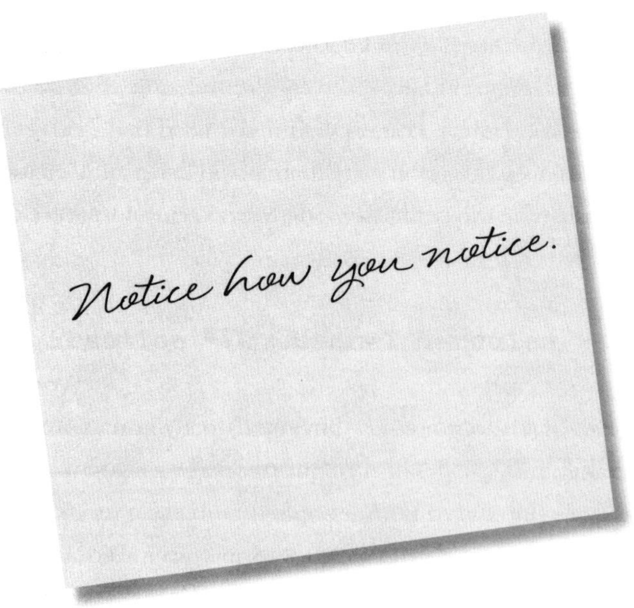

How do *you* perceive the world? How does the world come through your senses, bounce off your experiences, resonate through your emotions? The more conscious you can become of these subtle processes, the more you can know and develop your voice. Get curious about the limitations of your instrument and you'll begin to really find your voice.

Prompt: Notice How You Notice

Noticing helps you discover the uniqueness of your limitations and how they shape and direct your work. Like resistance, our limitations give us something to push against, something to push off of. Once you become aware of your "limitations," you can work with them in a positive way.

Step One: Spend five days noticing everything yellow in the world as you go about your daily life. Keep a running list of all the yellow things you see. There's no need to describe or philosophize or create a poem. Just notice and list: *Sunflower in vacant lot*; *cereal bowl*; *wife's rain boots*. And please—even if you see a yellow thing that strikes you as spectacular, *do not write while driving*. Seriously.

Step Two: Save your list for use in Practice #27.

Step Three: Notice how you noticed. At the end of the five days, spend a few minutes exploring each of the following questions in writing.

- Was there more yellow in the world than you expected? Less?
- Did you see things for the first time that you've driven or walked past every day for years?
- Did it wake you up? Slow you down?
- Did the color start to get on your nerves?

- Did you get hung up on what was "real" yellow and what was really orange or green?

Bonus Prompts: Other Ways to Practice Noticing

Notice vocal rhythms, tics, and patterns in others and then notice them in yourself.

Finish the sentence "Today I noticed . . ." or "Lately I've been noticing . . ." as many different ways as you can.

Spend a day just noticing which sensory organ you're most dependent on and which you use the least.

Notice what attracts or repels you. Try the sentence starters "I'm attracted to . . ." and "I'm repelled by . . ."

Notice what makes you curious. Try the sentence starter "I'm curious about . . ."

Notice what slows you down or speeds you up, what takes your energy or replenishes it.

Notice your beliefs, superstitions, opinions, and interests. Trace them back to their formation. From what teaching, relationship, or experience did that belief originate?

Notice sounds you hear every day or sounds that get on your nerves.

Notice what people are holding in their hands.

Notice the texture of what you're touching.

Notice your emotional reaction to what you're tasting.

Notice how your brain works. What is it good at? What derails it? What vitamins and foods best support its function? Does it like logic? Puzzles? Is it prone to rumination, fantasy, daydreaming? Does it prefer complexity? Abstraction? Or is it more attracted to the literal, physical world? Your brain is where all your perceptions are processed and delivered, so it pays to notice it.

15

Gifts—Picking and Choosing

Hike Your Own Hike / Be an Eager Receiver

For much of my life, when it came to gift-giving, anxiety got me coming and going. I agonized about finding just the right thing or spending just the right amount. A gift had to *mean* something, or *say* something, damn it. A gift was how you let someone know they mattered. But what if they mattered more to you than you did to them? What if you couldn't afford the gift that would make them feel valued? It was bad enough before Martha Stewart came along with her needle-felted handmade pillows and block-printed wrapping paper, raising the bar impossibly high.

And then there was receiving: the disturbing sense that a particular someone didn't get me at all—I mean, a subscription to *Glamour* magazine? Or, God forbid, the gift doesn't appear at all because the giver spaced on the anniversary or, how horrible, my *birthday*. Or, even worse, they remembered but left it to the last minute, and now they're acting like taking me to lunch was the plan all along, and I'm going to have to act like I don't know they forgot.

Worst of all for me was when I had to find a gift for a kid:

1. He already has three of those.
2. If the gift is not cool, the disdain is *right there.*

Then my niece, Camille, came along. No matter what I gave her—a coloring book, earrings, a fireman's hat, a bag of water balloons—she got so excited. She'd tremble and make little rising *eeeeeee* sounds as she undid the bow and peeled back the paper. She'd unwrap the package, peek in, and say, "No *way*!" She'd jump up and down, hugging whatever it was. "No way, Aunt Deb! No *way*!"—like it was an airplane ticket to Paris and not a packet of wildflower seeds. Every time. No matter what.

Not only did she restore the joy of giving gifts for me, but she showed me a much better way to receive.

Practice #26: Hike Your Own Hike

Up until age five, I thought all gifts were equally thrilling. Then I entered the school system, and it became clear that there were gifts and then there were *gifts*. It was especially apparent when we returned from Christmas vacation—a few kids would have received a serious upgrade to the latest fashions, toys, and gadgets, and some other kids would just look drawn and tired, like all they got was a few extra raisins in their oatmeal and a lot of family drama. And Valentine's Day? I don't know how they do it now, but when I was in school, we delivered cards to the desks of the kids we liked. The size of your valentine pile was directly proportional to your worth as a human being.

The girl who had the biggest valentine pile was Katie. She was blond, pretty, and Barbie feminine. She never got sweaty at recess, never returned from lunch with grape jelly on her chin. Her parents were wealthy and involved, and she was smart, and—what really drove me nuts—she was nice. She was the stick against which I measured my own gifts and found them wanting. I would never get straight As because math snarled my brain. Boys would never look at me like that. I would always get sweaty at recess and have grape jelly on my chin or my shirt or in my hair. My valentine pile would never be that big.

Our brains are geared for comparison. It's necessary to see how things are similar or different so that we don't mistake poisonous plants for medicinal ones or friendly people for hostile ones. But things go awry when we let comparison run the whole show.

In the workshops that I teach, writers and artists do timed exercises and read them aloud. When they aren't given the opportunity to think or compose, their voices are unchecked, and two things happen: 1) It's impossible to tell the experienced pros from the newbies. 2) Everyone's voice is nakedly unique, so that if you took the names off the papers and mixed them up you'd still be able to identify the authors.

In every workshop, without exception, I can expect each writer to confess their deep admiration for some other writer's voice. "Why is he even taking a workshop? If I could write like that, I'd be set." The lean writers love the wordy writers. The emotional writers love the dry writers. The wistful writers love the jaunty writers.

The problem with this is twofold. First, eyeballing the gifts of others prevents us from unwrapping, much less cultivating, our own. Second, the value of one creative virtue can't be defined by comparison with another. Hercules's ability to slay monsters is no more or less valuable than the balladeer's ability to enlighten and inspire the masses with tales of the demigod's adventures.

When my husband hiked the Appalachian Trail for the second time, he was twenty years older than the first time. In his midforties, he not only felt competitive with the other (mostly younger) hikers but he compulsively tried to keep up with his younger self. Trying to measure up to either or both, he immediately injured his ankle. "Hike your own hike" is a common refrain on the trail, and Chris spent the next two thousand miles rediscovering, for the first time, what his hike was.

It took me quite a while to realize that not being dainty and extroverted like Katie did not mean I was doomed to a life of lonely obscurity. Likewise, defying the creative stereotype doesn't mean you can't share your creative gifts. You don't have to be tortured or disturbed. You don't have to be dreamy or messy or bohemian. You don't have to have had a terrible childhood or have a degree from NYU.

It's apples and oranges: my way, your way; my old way, my new way. Or apples and pine cones, really. If the Katies and the Herculeses and the old selves serve to inspire you to reach for more life, great. If they serve only to show you what you're not, then it's time to flip the comparison switch in your brain to the Off position and unwrap your own singular, unrepeatable current gifts.

Think about how your attitude toward giving and receiving material gifts reflects your attitude toward your creative gifts: if every word that you receive onto the page is a disappointment, if every image and idea means something about your worth, if you compare each sentence against the ones created by your favorite authors, you're rejecting your gifts before you even unwrap them.

Prompt: Unwrap and Unpack Your Gifts

I don't want to suggest that there is such a thing as "being gifted," as if you're born with some creative trust fund that you can just cash in. Creative gifts are worked for and cultivated, just like athletic, intellectual, or business gifts. They're the nexus of your values, your voice, your biology, your formative experiences, and so much more, and as such, they're wildly complex. Before you can cultivate them and put them to good use, you must first unwrap them and understand them. Here are several prompts to get you looking in the right direction:

Step One: Write everything you know about your voice. In the last chapter, you launched a study of the limitations that make your sound unique. Now take it a step further and make an accounting of what you know about your voice to date—your actual voice or your creative voice, the literal or the ineffable. Whatever comes up: *My voice is raspy and papery. I got it from my father. It's the voice of dissent, but it works for lullabies, too.* Don't worry about nailing it or gaining deeper understanding. Just do the exercise for six minutes.

Step Two: Launch from the sentence starter "I'm drawn to . . ." and finish it as many ways as you can. Let it be obvious, trivial, earth-shattering, whatever it wants to be. Get it wrong. Write stupid stuff. *I'm drawn to the edge. I'm drawn to sunny climates. I'm drawn to shopping.* Write for six minutes.

Step Three: Launch from the sentence starter "I value . . ." and finish it as many ways as you can. *I value equal rights. I value a muscled butt. I value my job.* Write for six minutes.

Step Four: Launch from the sentence starter "I am from . . ." and let it take you where it will. When you run out of steam, come back to "I am from . . ." and start again. Be literal, geographical, genealogical, spiritual, energetic. Write down whatever comes up. Write for six minutes.

Practice #27: Be an Eager Receiver

I think it was during my first year of acting training that the conservatory hired a director named Joseph Chaikin to teach a workshop. He was a theater legend in his own time, a brilliant and beloved director who started The Open Theater in the sixties and expanded the experimental theater movement.

Joe was born with a heart condition and had recently suffered a stroke during one of his open-heart surgeries, which caused him to have aphasia, an injury to the parts of the brain that control language.

You would think that aphasia would be career-ending for a theater director. Every word Joe said, he had to fight for. Sometimes he said nearly the right word, but not quite, so that you had to decipher the meaning. Sometimes the mistake enhanced the meaning. He likened aphasia to receiving the word with its letters reversed or rearranged.

"Say your full name backward, starting with your last," he said.

Faces scrunched and eyes were raised ceilingward as we worked to unbuild and rebuild our names. Joe surveyed the room as one by one we sounded out our backward names. It took me longer than I would've expected to come up with "Notron Neaj Harobed."

Joe's problem wasn't with thinking; his mind was as brilliant as it always had been. The problem was with putting his thoughts into words. If he was going to share those thoughts, he couldn't waste energy rejecting one word in favor of a better one. He would do better to welcome whatever word was offered and make the best possible use of it. In this manner, over time, Joe rehabilitated his brain to the point that no one would guess he'd ever suffered an injury.

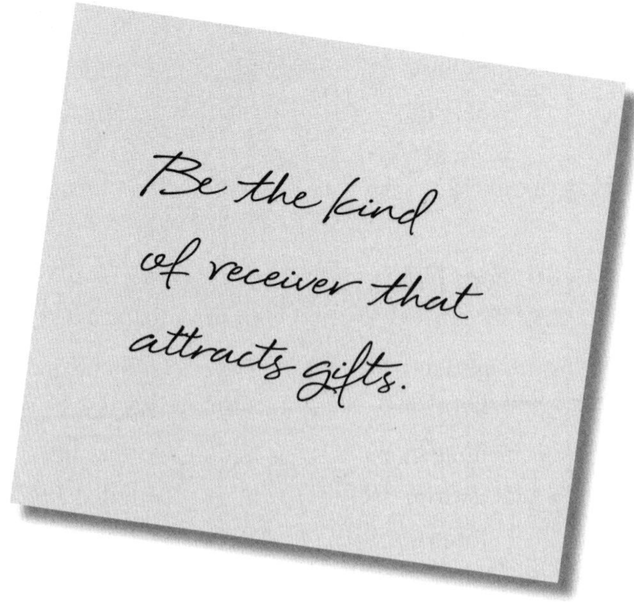

Be the kind
of receiver that
attracts gifts.

Can you receive your words, images, and ideas as the precious gifts that they are? Can you receive your life experiences, whether painful or joyful, as gifts to your art? Your daily interactions and observations, even if they bore or aggravate you, are gifts to your art. Your particular way of perceiving and expressing those experiences and interactions is the gift you have to give through your art and it, too, is precious, not for its comparative value but for its incomparable singularity.

Even your limitations are gifts. As discussed in the chapter on voice, limitations are what create your sound.

Rejecting your gifts, burdening them with your expectations, or taking them personally will result in diminishing returns. An eager and welcoming attitude toward your gifts will result in wealth and variety. You may not understand right away how to make use of some of the words and ideas that show up on the page, but if you receive them with curiosity and a sense of possibility you're more likely to discern their potential. If not, the worst that will have happened is a page full of unused words. (And it's not like you have to find space for them in your closet or garage, or worry about the giver spotting them at the local thrift shop.)

We feel the need to be tough with ourselves and judge our creations harshly, lest others do it for us. But, what if, instead, you receive your creative gift with breathless excitement?

Prompt: The Perfect Gift

Even though improvisation class did me a world of good in acting school, I barely survived the nerves. But here's an improv exercise I like because it can be done in the privacy of your own home (or writing space). I adapted it from an exercise in a book called *Impro for Storytellers*, by Keith Johnstone, which is a rich resource for writers and artists.

Step One: Give.

1. Recruit a friend, partner, or child to do the exercise with you.
2. Get on your feet. This exercise doesn't work sitting down.
3. Player A (that's you) pretends to give a gift to Player B, stating out loud what the gift is: "Here, I got you a flower." (Note: The gift is pretend; therefore, it's invisible.) Say the first thing that comes into your head, even if the first thing that comes into your head is "cotton ball" or "skyscraper."
4. Player B receives the gift with delight. Pretend delight is fine for our purposes. "Thank you! It's exactly what I wanted!" Every gift. No exceptions. No need to explain why the gift is perfect. Just receive it eagerly.
5. Switch. Player B pretends to give a gift to Player A. Player A receives the gift with delight. No exceptions.
6. Repeat, giving gifts back and forth for three minutes or more.

Important: No matter what you receive, no matter whether it's something you want or something you're downright frightened of, act as though you're delighted with the gift.

Step Two: Receive.

1. Repeat the game, but this time the receiver says what the gift is. Player A pretends to give a gift, but doesn't say what it is: "Here, I got you . . . this." Player A might mime the weight, size, or shape of the gift if he's so inclined.
2. Player B, taking his cue from Player A, says the first thing that comes to mind: "Oh! Thank you for this cartoon/tractor/piglet!"
3. All gifts are received with delight: "It's exactly what I wanted!" No exceptions.
4. Keep exchanging gifts for three minutes.

Important: Givers, resist the temptation to "help" the receiver "see" the gift by giving hints. Receivers, resist the urge to guess correctly or come up with something interesting.

Step Three: The gift that keeps on giving.

1. Find your "List of Yellow Things" from Practice #25.
2. Choose a yellow item from the list that you would like to spend a little time with, for any reason whatsoever. A bus, a daisy, the pee in the toilet—whatever catches your attention.
3. Write everything you know about that chosen yellow item (remember, it doesn't matter whether you know much about it at all). Keep your pen moving. Don't worry about doing it justice or making it interesting. See if you can receive the words with gratitude as they come through your pen. Write for six minutes.

Step Four: Free gift.

1. Read your writing from step three aloud to your gift-giving partner. As you do, "give" it to them with an open and generous heart.
2. When you're finished reading, your partner will say, "Thank you, that's exactly what I wanted!"
3. Switch and repeat.

Step Five: Locate your gratitude. Write a thank-you note, just as you would for a birthday or wedding gift, expressing gratitude for your creativity and for the creative gifts that come to you and through you. Write for six minutes or more.

16

Legitimacy—Getting Real

Make a Seat at the Table

Actors are prone to the anxiety dream commonly referred to as "the actor's nightmare" in which they are urgently needed on stage but don't know their lines and probably aren't wearing any pants. I continued to have this dream with annoying regularity long after I'd quit acting.

The truth is, I was prone to fraught and anxious dreams for much of my life. To name a few, there were the ones where I could only see sideways, the ones where I was being chased but could only run in slo-mo, the ones where I was possessed, and the ones where I was driving a car with no brakes, no acceleration, or no windshield wipers in a bad storm. I even had a dream where I was trying to drive a car from the backseat. And then there were the ones where I had an important meeting, but I just couldn't find something appropriate to wear. Oh, and I can't leave out the one where I have to go to the bathroom, but I can't find one with a door. I'd gotten to feeling embarrassed about how obvious my subconscious was—*I get it, okay? I get that I can't see a way forward, that I feel like I'm not in control, not in the driver's seat, don't feel ready, don't have a safe place to "release." Do we have to go over and over it?*

But there was one recurring dream that really disturbed me: the baby dream. I would be at the grocery store and come across an infant, you know, just lying on a shelf next to the cereal, and I'd realize, "Oh my God. This is *my* baby. How could I have forgotten that I had a baby?! I must have left it here last time I went shopping." Or I might find it under my sink or in the clothes hamper, sometimes crying, often listless from neglect. Sometimes the dream would have a different spin and it would be a bird I'd forgotten to care for huddled on the floor of a cage, the food and water dishes empty. Always, the feeling of guilt and sadness was crushing—this innocent living being that I loved so much was in my charge, and I'd completely neglected it . . .

I haven't had the baby dream or the possession, chasing, or driving dreams in ages. Not since I started calling myself a writer.

Practice #28: Make a Seat at the Table

I thought there would be a moment of arrival, a point at which I'd know that I was a real writer. It didn't happen when I got my first play produced or my first review in a major paper, or even when I signed a contract for a movie option. I'd be a real writer when I made my living at it, I figured. And then: I'd be a real writer when I won awards, and then when I worked with famous people, and then when I myself was famous.

Can you imagine refusing the title of "parent" until your child can prove to the world that your parenting skills are worthy of recognition? No. You call yourself a parent the minute a child is in your care.

I wanted my writing to prove itself. I wanted it to earn a seat at my table—*show me you're a winner.* It's so crazy to think about it now. I mean, *winner*? I don't even like competition. It makes me cry, and that's not hyperbole. I remember the first time it happened: I was playing cards with my grandparents and my brother. We were using dried beans for poker chips because we were on a camping trip. I kept my face in the shadow of the kerosene lantern to hide my tears because, at seven, I knew I was too old to be a sore loser. But I hated that there were only the two options: if someone won, someone else had to lose. For someone to have a lot of beans, you had to end up with just a few.

"That's just the way the world works, kiddo," the adults would say.

But it's not. There are certain human pursuits that can't be legitimized by winning, no matter how hard we try.

I had a friend in high school who had an entire wall of his bedroom devoted to the ribbons, awards, and trophies he'd won. Whether on the field or in the classroom, he crushed all competition, brought home the proof, and put it on the wall. But it was never enough. It never brought him any closer to his distant father.

Ask not what your writing can do for you; ask what you can do for your writing.

There are aspects of being human that have no system for measurement and can only be legitimized in the doing of them: creating, parenting, loving, discovering, and playing, to name a few. And they are the most important things we do.

My baby and bird dreams were a cry for help from the part of me that longed to be fully adopted and cherished so that, in return, it could bring joy and meaning to my life. It was saying, *I'm here, I'm yours, I'm extraordinary. Care for me. Make me flourish.*

Are you giving your writing the least of your love and energy, while wishing it to earn contracts, cash, prizes, recognition, monuments? Okay, fine, maybe competition and ambition keeps you in the chair. But can your creations truly shine when your creativity doesn't feel it even has a place at your table?

How do you know you're a real writer? You know it because you're writing.

You don't need to go out and get a doctorate to legitimize your right to work at your craft. Creativity is the most legitimate and valuable part of any human being, from the get-go. It elevates our existence. It's our crowning virtue.

And, hey, I get it. The part of me that loves my creativity and knows it's the best thing in my life is not immune to the inner-critic part of me that rolls its eyes and says, "Honey, that art stuff was cute when you were little, but now it's getting embarrassing."

Approval, praise, awards, money, degrees—it's all wonderful when it happens, but it doesn't prove that your creative efforts are legitimate. Legitimacy is inherent. It's just scary to claim it, because it means so much.

It has to be you. No one, no matter how smart or powerful, can declare you a real artist. No matter how much evidence you gather, it will only be anecdotal. By the same token, no one can prove that you are, or are *not*, an artist. So instead of collecting evidence that can never add up to proof, claim it. Reach down to the very root of yourself and draw up that deep-seated truth. Claim your creativity as a fully vested part of your life. Make it the most important part of your life.

Prompt: Formally Adopt Your Creativity

After my widowed friend accepted the proposal of her second husband, he proposed again, on bended knee, to her daughter. "Molly, I promise to be the best father I can be for you. Will you be my lawfully adopted daughter?" This formal and respectful proposal let the little girl know she was not a bystander in her mother's marriage but part of the reason for it.

Step One: Rescue. Close your eyes and picture yourself in a house. Whatever comes up is fine—your childhood home, a *Downton Abbey*–type manor in the throes of a party, a city apartment, whatever. Now go from room to room until you find your creativity. Maybe you know where to look and what to look for. Maybe you have no idea. Maybe it's in the pantry. Maybe it's in some far corner of the attic. It might take a while, but don't give up. At some point, you open a door and there it is. As soon as this happens, hold that image, open your eyes, and write what you see: Is it male, female, young, old, an animal, a creature? What is its manner? Is it busy with a task, or singing, or resting? Is it serene, is it frenetic? Don't worry if it feels forced or like you're making it up. Write for six minutes.

Step Two: Reclaim. Think of a comfortable place to be with your creativity—the kitchen table or the living room sofa, for instance. Sit your creativity down and tell it you'd like to adopt it as a legitimate and full-fledged part of you. Explain that you want to eliminate the distance between you and take up your role in the partnership with much more intention. Find out what its needs, tendencies, and interests are so that you can support it in becoming its fullest, most robust self. Write for at least six minutes.

Bonus Prompts: Other Ways to Get Legitimate

Start referring to yourself as a writer, artist, dancer, inventor, baker. Claim that. Say it as confidently as you would say that you're thirty years old, or that you're a Californian, or a teacher, or the son of a salesman, or a nature lover, or a runner.

Pay attention to your creativity as you would with a child or partner, noticing what it needs—time, attention, a walk in the fresh air. Would your writing benefit from vitamins? Leafy greens? More exercise? Your creativity might need to go for a drive or get to a yoga class. Or it might need to write.

Acknowledge what's working in your writing. Underline and highlight words and passages that feel like they have energy or potential.

Do anything that makes you feel strong, brave, and awake.

Stop doing things that weaken or deplete you.

Tell your friends and family about how your writing is going and let them know how they can support you.

Notice how your writing space is or is not serving your writing efforts. Make adjustments.

III

Resistance is ~~Futile~~ Fertile

Let the Sunshine In

Most of us are dogged by an internal critic. You know the one: that voice in your head that harps on your flaws and mistakes and your impending failure. You do your best to tune it out and keep on truckin', but it just doesn't quit. However, like most hecklers, if you turn the glaring spotlight around and put them in the hot seat, they aren't quite so bold.

17

Inner Critic—Nagging and Doubting

List and Separate / Get the Story / Create a Hostile Environment

I was writing at my local café. I had my earbuds in but no music playing, which signaled my disinterest in socializing but didn't prevent me from eavesdropping.

At the next table, a woman in her sixties tapped steadily on her keyboard. I tapped steadily on mine in solidarity and friendly competition. A younger woman, in her thirties maybe (who can tell anymore how old anyone under fifty is, especially in Southern California?), flounced into the empty chair next to my "writing partner" and threw a hug and a kiss on her—a niece? A goddaughter? They smiled and talked about their respective tea choices, the weather, and their outfits, and then the young one gestured to the laptop. "What are you working on?"

"I'm writing a book. Stories from my life."

The youngster rolled her eyes. "*Everyone's* writing a book these days. It's a *thing*."

My pretend writing partner gently shut the lid on her laptop but continued in cheerful conversation on other topics.

I was stunned. *Oh, my poor, dear writing partner, you can't unring that bell.* That eye roll—it was in her head now, where she couldn't get away from it.

Damn, I thought. *I've probably rung that bell for someone.* In fact, I know I have. In my teens and twenties, I rolled my eyes a lot. I was a self-hating creative. Even in acting school, where all my friends were actors, directors, and writers, I held an old blue-collar belief that art wasn't *real* work. But I didn't even know this about myself until I made my first tentative writing attempts and my inner critic came screaming out of the shadows, hair on fire. Only then was I able to see how toxic it was; only then was I able to stop it from coming out of my face to snipe at others.

Once I could see and hear it clearly, I recognized my inner critic immediately. It was my stepfather. Or, not my stepfather, but an aspect of him, the aspect that was all about discipline, working hard, and above all, humility. And you know what's not humble? Thinking you have something so important to say that it's worth writing down. I mean, how could I write with this thought hijacking my brain?

My inner "stepdad" believed that creativity was for people who thought they were somehow too good for real work. Per my actual stepdad, "real work" meant wearing protective gear and having calluses. It meant ground-in dirt that couldn't be removed without special soap. If it didn't risk injury or at least dehydration, if it didn't give you an ulcer, you weren't working hard enough. Just like my real stepdad, my inner stepdad was never without a box of Maalox in his shirt pocket.

I didn't actually believe that creativity was an affront to the working class, but I'd internalized this voice so that it came to feel like it was mine. Once I really tuned in, though, I heard all the voices that were woven in with my stepfather's: the cool girl who smirked at my clothes, the teacher who made an example of me for speaking out of turn, the mean boss whose radar I was careful to fly under, and on and on. And now they spoke as one, a Greek chorus of judgment.

Maybe the bell couldn't be unrung, but I could stop swinging from the rope like Quasimodo. I didn't have to keep that noise going. And I sure as hell didn't have to be the eye roller who rang somebody else's bell.

Practice #29: List and Separate

You weren't born with a disparaging voice in your head. You, as a little baby, did not gaze down at your legs and think, "Man, what is with these fat ankles? Hideous! I can't speak the language. Food goes everywhere when I eat. Oh, come on, did I just soil myself *again*? Why can't I get it together?!"

No, inner critics are not part of the basic package. They're non-native. They are invasive, slipping into your psyche when a teacher uses shame to motivate you, or when someone insecure wants to one-up you, or when somebody sells their product by making you fear your difference, and on and on.

I know it feels like your voice, your thoughts, but I promise you: what you are hearing are other people's fears, passed on to you like a virus.

Think about it this way: do you want to write? Yes, you do. Does your inner critic want you to write? No, it does not. Does it help you write? No. In fact, it hinders you. So, maybe you and your inner critic are not one and the same.

The voice of my inner critic was inexhaustible. I couldn't write a note to inform my roommate that I'd had some of her almond milk without it weighing in on the quality of the prose. It was exasperating. If a real person were dogging my heels, picking apart my looks and my decisions, telling me I would never realize my dreams, reminding me of every misstep I'd ever made in my life, I would get rid of them. If they were anything like my inner critic, I'd probably push them in front of a train.

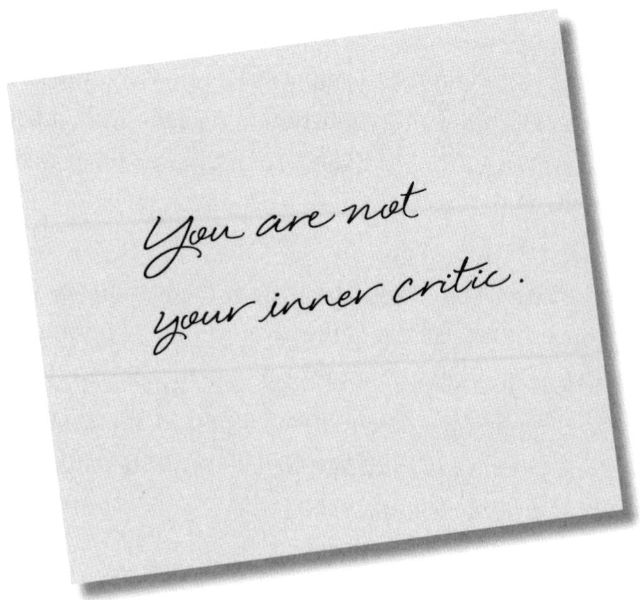
You are not
your inner critic.

I read everything I could find about how to deal with inner critics, and everything was focused toward "silencing" or "killing" them. Well, I'm sorry, but I can't silence my inner critic, because it communicates via my thoughts. They don't make earplugs that keep out thoughts—at least not yet. And I can't kill something that's not real, not even with a train.

In fact, ignoring and fighting the inner critic made it worse. Have you ever noticed what happens when you ignore a bully? They talk louder, right? They throw spitballs and amp up the abuse. But shower them with your rapt attention and it takes the steam right out of their pipes.

I decided to try the sunshine cure and just blast my inner critic with light. I got myself good and curious, put on my protective hazmat suit, threw open the doors, and invaded its toxic territory. I got it talking and listened—really listened.

Prompt: Let the Sunshine In

Important: If you begin the prompts in this practice, you must continue on and do the rest of the practices as well. To leave it before the process is complete will most likely aggravate your inner-critic issues rather than ease them.

Step One: Describe your naked body in as much detail as you can. I know it's uncomfortable, but to draw your inner critic out, you need the right bait. Anyway, the more you get comfortable with being uncomfortable, the more you'll write, because writing is uncomfortable. Now, in the privacy of your own mind, take off your clothes and imagine you're standing in front of a full-length mirror in a well-lit room. Look at your reflection and describe what you see in as much detail as you can. Write for six minutes.

Step Two: Change your point of view. In your imagination, turn from the mirror and find yourself in full view of someone who adores you. This person finds you beautiful in all your wonderful complexity. In fact, the more *you* you are, the more this person adores you. Have you ever loved anyone in such a way that their crooked teeth or love handles or dimpled ass or gnarled and spotted hands all added up to something you craved to be near? I'm talking *that* kind of devotion. If you don't currently have such a person in your life, or even if you do, feel free to invent the adoring presence of your dreams. Write in the first person, from your admirer's point of view, describing your body for six minutes.

Step Three: Take stock. This exercise exposes the restrictions your inner critic places on your vision. When you look at yourself, if you see only what needs to be fixed, you aren't seeing the complexity of what's really there. These vision restrictions can carry over into how you see aspects of your writing. So, getting a handle on your inner critic isn't just about your self-esteem, you see—it's about the writing.

Don't worry, though. Even if your inner critic gave you hell during the exercise, you're already turning the tables on it. You might have gotten some pushback for writing something nice about your body, even if it was from another point of view. It may have gotten nasty about your "flaws." You might even feel a little shaky. Remind yourself that the intention was to flush out your inner critic, kind of like when the hero gets the villain monologuing to lure him into a trap. So if you got your inner critic going, that's good. The bait worked.

Once the inner critic is stirred up, shift the focus off yourself and onto it.

What are the specific tactics or tones it uses to manipulate you—passive aggression, shame, snobbishness, perfectionism? List any methods your inner critic might employ to inhibit or discourage you. Write for three minutes.

What is your inner critic's general emotional state? Fury? Melodrama? Anxiety? Cold, controlled anger? Describe the vibe in the inner-critic sanctum. Write for three minutes.

Step Four: Listen. Make a list of every unhelpful or limiting thing you've ever heard your inner critic say about you, your body, your intellect, your life choices, your habits or creative efforts. Then make its day by inviting it to say all the things you've *refused* to hear. Get it talking by letting it know you're *interested*. Cultivate some real curiosity: "All right, I'm all ears. I'm finally going to listen." It's okay if it gets personal, insulting, ugly. (We'll deal with that later.) Let it get good and whipped up: *Who do you think you are, you should be focusing on your kids, you're selfish, you're lazy, you need to lose ten pounds, I just don't want you to get hurt.* Don't respond or defend. Just list. Write for six minutes.

Was there anything that felt too painful to write? If you are able, go ahead and write it now. Do this in defiance of that limiting force that would have you just sit there and take it.

Note: Whenever I do this exercise, I'm shocked to see what meanness I've been walking around with. But more importantly, whenever I run this exercise with a group of writers and artists, they are amazed to discover that everyone in the room, without exception, is carrying this old, toxic junk around inside them, too. No one is the biggest basket case in the room. Additionally, my students feel compassion for one another, and this creates some space for self-compassion. Every human being over six years of age is walking around with some version of this internal meanness. It's normal.

Step Five: Take names. Whether you have a single inner critical voice or, like me, a Greek chorus, it's important to remember that it's constructed of every limiting comment, expression, or image you've been exposed to. Now it's time to deconstruct. Go through the list of comments from step three and see if you can figure out where each one originated. Write all the possible names of the speakers of these unspeakable things. They may be real people who left a mark: *the bully, Mrs. Patterson, my former agent, Mom, Grandpa, Aunt Charlotte* . . . Then again, they may not be real or even human: *the Winner, the Red Pen, Skinny Lingerie Model, the Nose.* Sometimes they come from books and TV: *Martha Stewart, the Nike Commercial, the Well-Adjusted Sitcom Family.* It might be that the entire panel of judges from *America's Got Talent* is in there. Maybe you only met them once, like that guy who flipped you off on the freeway and mouthed, "Idiot!" Write a name by each critical comment to identify the source, whether it's a real person or an imaginary "friend." Save this information for use in Practice #30.

Important: If the comments came from loved ones, don't let this worry you. It is simply a *shred* or *aspect* of your loved one. It's not a summary judgment of your mother's character to attribute a limiting comment to her.

Note: One valuable function of an inner critic is that, in the same way that fear illuminates the edge, they tell you where the treasure is. They are the guardians at the gate, barking, snarling, loosing arrows, lopping off heads, and keeping the treasure locked up. The bigger and badder the guards, the bigger and better the treasure. Notice when your inner critic gets really red in the face, nervous, or angry. Whatever you're writing when this happens will probably take you directly to creative gold, if you can brave the blustering.

Practice #30: Get the Story

When my acting training ended, I wasn't quite ready to face the looming task of starting my career. My classmate Gillian suggested a road trip to the Grand Canyon and then up to Cedar City to see a friend perform in the Utah Shakespeare Festival. It sounded like a great way to put off the future for a few weeks.

"Let's take the 33 and swing by Taft," Gillian proposed.

Taft is the town I grew up in, an oil town in the most desolate part of the San Joaquin Valley. I couldn't imagine why she'd want to go there. I didn't.

"Because it's where you're from," she said. "I've never known anyone from there. I want to see it. I want to see the oil wells and the tumbleweeds. Maybe a dust devil. Are those real?"

She's from Santa Barbara.

My stepfather still lived in Taft. He'd stayed and remarried after the divorce, and my mom and I had moved to the coast. I hadn't talked to him in seven or eight years. Maybe it was time.

"Why not," I said.

Gillian toured the oil museum while my stepfather took me to lunch at the Sno-White Drive-In. We made small talk for a while, concentrating on our overstuffed burgers. Then, without warning, he just up and apologized.

"I know what I put you through was . . . none of you did anything to deserve all that."

He was talking about his anger. It had two modes: fuming that built to hitting and discipline with a side of shame. Assessing, defusing, and avoiding his anger was the full-time occupation of our family. It had set my nerves to permanent hypervigilance mode, and was paying out in an array of health and relationship problems.

"That was a bad time for me," he said. "I was always worried about money. There was never enough money, and I was under so much stress. I didn't know how to handle it."

I'd spent my childhood hiding in my room because of *money worries*? How did that have anything to do with me? I was a kid; I couldn't be accountable for the size of his paycheck. What kind of apology was this?

Then he told me about his childhood, working his way from Oklahoma to California with his family, picking fruit. He lived in abject poverty, sharing shoes with his siblings, working long hours, taking schooling in bits and pieces. As the oldest, he was responsible for his siblings as well as earning his share, and he took the brunt of his father's fears and frustration in the form of regular beatings.

Jesus, I thought, *Mr.* Grapes of Wrath *is sitting across from me.* All those iconic pictures of gaunt mothers and dusty children . . . In all my efforts to avoid him, I'd managed to learn nothing about him.

It must have pushed all his buttons to have this nervous, sensitive, math-challenged kid on his hands when he knew what a keen edge was needed to survive. And my brother, with his undiagnosed dyslexia—from where my stepdad sat, that looked a lot like laziness, and lazy people starved.

Forgiving him was a longer process, but hearing his story allowed me to see that he was human. With this injection of complexity, I wasn't chained to him anymore. My hurt and fear had heat-welded me to him, I realized, and kept me in a struggle that was long over—a struggle I couldn't resolve because it wasn't about me. It had never been about me.

I didn't say much at the time, but if I could go back, I guess I'd tell him how he'd affected me, how set back I felt, how I'd been out in the world a little bit and seen that people can be happy, can be vulnerable and make mistakes and they aren't struck by disaster. But in telling him, I would just have been telling myself. We weren't going to become great friends at this point. In fact, it was just the opposite: now we could finally part ways.

Afterward, I drove to the West Kern Oil Museum to pick up Gillian. She sat under the iconic wooden oil derrick, surrounded by guys—back then, Taft was disproportionately populated by young men who'd been lured by the oil field's high wages. It was a buffet of military tats, Wranglers, mullets, and wallet chains.

Gillian climbed into the car, waving good-bye to her new friends. "They all have such good manners."

"Well, what now?" I asked.

"I'm dying to see a swamp cooler. Do you know where to find one?"

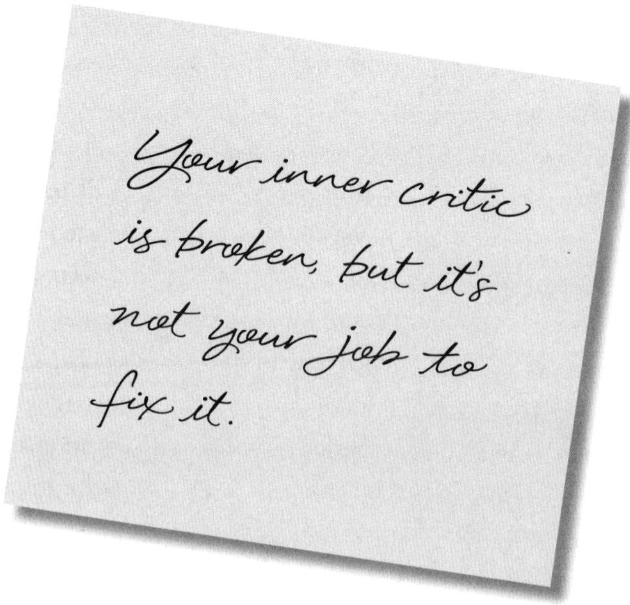

Your inner critic
is broken, but it's
not your job to
fix it.

Even the most miserable, pain-in-the-ass person has a story. We just rarely get to know what it is because we're too busy trying to get away from him or her.

Highly critical people, bullies, and tyrants pay their pain forward instead of processing it for story gold the way *you're* doing. Unprocessed hurt drives them to play out their inner drama in the outside world, and they go around all Johnny Appleseed, planting their pain wherever they find fertile soil. And sensitive people, creative people—we are soft. We are fertile soil. So for the sake of our creativity, we have to be very *aware* if we are to avoid becoming a flowering orchard of everybody else's junk.

You may not be able to forgive a particularly nasty detractor just on the virtue of having heard her story. But perhaps you can take her less to heart, knowing that her negativity is not about you; often, this awareness is enough to give you some creative breathing room.

Prompt: Get the Story

Look over your list of names from step five of Practice #29's prompt and choose an inner critic to work with.

Step One: Map it (see p. 223). Now that you've drawn it out of the shadows, take a good look at your inner critic. Is it all teeth and claws, just like you thought it was? Or is it some twisted version of your stepdad, your frenemy, or a girl who rejected you? Take a minute to get a clear image. Where do you carry this inner critic in your body? Maybe you experience it as a tightness, an ache, a heaviness. Put your hand on this part of your body. What comes up—images, colors, sensations, memories? Use this information to get even clearer, and then draw your inner critic, or the feeling of your inner critic, on your body map.

Step Two: Write everything you know about your inner critic. Continue working with the same inner critic. What does he/she/it look like, act like, say? Include habits, gestures, clothes, characteristics: *he drives an Austin Healey, smokes in the bathtub, kicks cats, smells of pine sap*—anything that comes to you. If it feels too tame or contrived or blamey or angry, that's all fine. Don't let your inner critic give you grief about how you write about your inner critic. Write for six minutes.

Note: If the inner critic is someone you know—your grandmother, a friend, a teacher—remember that this is the inner-critic version of that person, who may or may not have much in common with their real-life counterpart.

Step Three: Write your inner critic's autobiography. I like to use a variation of an exercise from Deena Metzger's book *Writing for Your Life* to help loosen the inner critic's stranglehold. Imagine he/she/it has a fully realized life, separate from your own. Take dictation as he spills his life story, memories, opinions, philosophy, hopes, regrets, relationships, etc. If he tries to talk about you, steer him back to his own story. What's his economic situation? Who are his parents? Turning points in his life? Hobbies? Musical tastes? Favorite book? The only thing this critic is not allowed to talk about is *you*. It's important that you keep him on the subject of himself. Since you're taking dictation, write in the first person from the inner critic's point of view: *I was born in Texas to an insurance salesman and a failed TV starlet.* Remember, the best way to get someone talking is to be genuinely curious. It doesn't have to feel authentic, or like you're channeling the essence of your inner critic. Don't think: just be curious and write for six minutes or more.

Step Four: Answer the following questions in writing:

Notice how you feel. How did your inner critic's story affect you?

Read back through your writing and underline any surprising revelations

or unexpected details—anything that feels like new information. What do you now know about this inner critic that you didn't know before?

Through this story, can you sense the source of his pain? What is it?

Are you the source of his pain? Were you ever?

Now that you know your inner critic better, you can decide whether he's qualified to be your inner critic. Can he help you make your work better, or is he just keeping you from doing it?

Note: If this practice is stirring up more critical voices, that's normal, and even positive. It means they aren't getting away with their passive-aggressive or subversive manipulation anymore. As you do this uncomfortable work of drawing each inner critic out from behind the curtain, you can take solace in knowing that his or her story contains fabulous raw material from which you can create an endless array of complex and compelling antagonists.

Practice #31: Create a Hostile Environment

I've heard it said that the best writers are their own worst critics. Okay, fine. Let's entertain the possibility of a positive function for the inner critic, because while some of them are just there to tear you down, there are those that seem genuine in their desire to help. They're on the same page with you about at least one thing—they want the work to be excellent, right?

Nuh-uh. Sorry. This kind of inner critic is even worse than the outright adversarial ones, because he manipulates you through your best intentions. He convinces you that he's the last and only real line of defense between you and total failure, humiliation, and financial ruin. He tells you he's the only one who really cares. He spins stories of terrible danger to frighten you so you'll hire him on as your security detail.

Your inner critic does not have your back.

Your inner critic is an expert on exactly nothing.

Maybe you feel a certain loyalty to your inner critic—after all, he's given you so much attention! Or maybe you're afraid that without your inner critic, you'll have no perspective on your work. If your inner critic wasn't there to tell you, "That sounds like a child wrote it," perhaps you would fall into a stupor of self-love and forget to strive for greatness.

The truth is, many of us think of the inner critic as the expert.

We harbor the belief that they know the *real* us—that they know us better than we know ourselves. This is the ultimate inner-critic trap.

It's okay to let go. The inner critic is a shred of someone else's brokenness that has made its home in your brain. I have to advise you not to put a shred of brokenness in charge of your most important and sacred activities.

If you have a codependent relationship with your inner critic, the dysfunction may feel like a kind of security. This is the toughest kind of inner critic to shake. But if you're ready to get free, the prompts below are designed to make him *want* to leave. The goal is to exasperate him with your appalling disregard for his sage council. Make him throw his hands up and say, "I give up! I can't do a thing with you! If you don't appreciate my support, then I'm leaving!"

And please remember, you don't have to take care of him through the breakup. He'll be fine.

Prompt: Piss Off Your Inner Critics

Step One: Single-syllable speed-write. Choose a topic. Anything will do—the tree outside your window, the cantaloupe you had for breakfast, your feet, your hair, anything. Now write everything you know about that topic—but use only one-syllable words. Feel free to invent new contractions or to abbreviate when convenient. Don't try to be clever. Just keep your pen moving. Write as fast as you can for six minutes.

Read back through the one-syllable speed-write and underline any words or phrases that you're drawn to. Did you accidentally find a fresh way to say something? Great! Your inner critic will hate that! Did your inner critic castigate you for not obeying the rules when you accidentally used a multisyllabic word? Underline those words as well to show your inner critic that you don't make progress without breaking rules and making mistakes.

Step Two: "Insults and Bad Words." Write a list of every insult, slur, or curse word you can think of. Include juvenile taunts (*butt face*), everyday cussing (*shit*, *damn*, *crap*), meanness (*thunder thighs*, *pizza face*), and slander (the more politically incorrect the better). Don't worry if nonsensical insults appear (*slackalump*, *rock looter*). Especially include those words and phrases that make you very uncomfortable. If there are any insults that you feel too nervous or embarrassed to write, stare right at your inner critic and write them extra large. Hopefully the inner critic who doesn't want you to get into trouble or ever offend anybody or sound immature or less intelligent than you really are will be really bothered by this exercise. Write for six minutes and know that you can burn it on the barbecue afterward.

Note: You may write a story with an unapologetically misogynistic, racist, epithet-spewing character in it. It's important for you to bring him to the page as he is, not as your inner critic thinks he should be: "You don't want anybody to know that you have someone that hateful in your mind!" You and I both know that your responsibility is to the story, not the inner critic. The "Insults and Bad Words" prompt is a great way to strengthen your ability to write what needs to be written rather than what represents you well.

Step Three: "Talents and Secret Powers." List everything you're good at: *rock climbing, cooking, selling, organizing, jumping really high, driving.* Are you good at calming people, making them laugh or feel loved? Be sure to list everything, whether or not it's something you'd bring up in polite society, such as being good at sex. Get specific. And then there are your secret powers—those things that are particular to you, possibly innate. For example, my mother can flip the bird with her toes. I had a friend who always won the raffle prize. Can you guess when it's going to rain? Can you fire people without hurting their feelings? Be aware of your inner critic trying to grab the pen with backhanded compliments like *really good at making bad decisions*. Keep it positive. If there's anything you feel really self-conscious about, write it extra large. Notice if there's any part of you that enjoys exploring your strengths. That's the part you want to be unified with. The part of you that's embarrassed—that's your inner critic. Take pleasure in making your inner critic uncomfortable. List for six minutes.

Bonus Prompts: Other Uses for the One-Syllable Speed-write

When you're truly stuck, the one-syllable speed-write makes it impossible to stay in whatever rut you've fallen into. Since you can't use the words you'd normally reach for, you're forced to find another way to express your thoughts.

When you've been struggling for the perfect way to say something for more than five minutes, do a one-syllable speed-write. It will shake your inner perfectionist off your tail.

When you need a fresh way to see something or someone, a one-syllable speed-write will force your pen out of known territory. The faster you go, the more you're likely to stumble onto something useful.

Other uses for "Talents and Secret Powers"

List the talents and secret powers of your characters to discover something unexpected about them.

When you need to give a toast or a tribute, write a love letter, or even a eulogy, first try doing the "Talents and Secret Powers" exercise for the person you're honoring.

18

Outer Critics—Feedback and Noise

Train Your Ears / Cull and Cultivate

After the first few showcase readings I had for my playwriting students, I started giving this speech beforehand:

"After the show, people will want to say nice things to you about your work. You will have the impulse to shoot them down. Check that impulse."

I had spent the previous post-show receptions listening to my writers responding to gushing praise with things like, "Oh, it was a mess. I could barely watch. I know I'm not Tom Stoppard or anything." They were heavily conditioned to deflect praise. The poor audience member would end up feeling like a putz for liking their play.

"Just say thank you," I'd tell them. "Say, 'I'm so glad you enjoyed it. Thank you so much for coming.' "

Dubious looks all around.

"No, seriously. Turn to each other and say it right now."

And I'd make them practice, so that they'd be able to override that knee-jerk instinct to shut down any positive responses to their work.

Practice #32: Train Your Ears

There is a school of thought that says if you listen to your good reviews, you must also listen to your bad ones. This is a little black and white for my taste. I think learning how to field criticism is a titch more complex than that.

In my experience, most artists don't have trouble letting in the negative criticism. In fact, we sponge it right up. When it comes to praise, though, we are less absorbent. There is a kind of artistic selective deafness that shuts out the positive feedback and seals in the negative. The more negative it is, the more deeply it penetrates.

A good friend of mine once told me she never gave any weight to positive feedback. "People say nice things out of obligation. You never know whether they really feel that way or if they're just afraid to say what they really think. But criticism, I mean, why would anyone say something negative unless it were true?"

Selective deafness
is not good for
your writing.

Okay, let's take that question at face value. People might say something negative about your work because:

* They're envious—consciously or not—that you're taking risks and expressing yourself while they are denying themselves any creative release.
* Your work inspired their frustrated inner writer to think of all the ways that *they* would tell the story if *they* were writing it.
* A character in your story reminded them of someone they detest.
* Your story opened their hearts, and they hate feeling vulnerable.
* Something in your story offended them personally or politically, and they can't distinguish between disagreeing with something and disliking something.
* They ate too much at dinner and have terrible gas and are just uncomfortable and cranky.
* They didn't understand your story, because they didn't listen carefully, because they were too distracted by all of the above.
* They want to sound smart.

I could fill many pages with this list. Negative feedback is often less carefully considered and more personally motivated than positive feedback.

You need wide-open ears. Listening is one of your greatest resources, and if you're tuning out half of what you hear, you're using that resource incorrectly. If you're averse to positive feedback, you'll never know what's working, where your particular creative power sits, and what's compelling about your particular voice. If you're hyper-focused on what's wrong in your writing, you may miss what's working. This is a real problem, because it leaves you with no foundation to build on.

But it's fraught, right? Compliments are tricky. There are obligatory compliments and backhanded compliments. Some compliments are given only to provoke a return compliment. What to take in? What to believe?

The first step to dealing productively with any kind of feedback is to notice *how* you're hearing it. Notice if you shut out positive feedback and pull in the negative, or vice versa.

The second is to understand *what* you're hearing.

Opinions: Likes and dislikes

The human mind wants to sort things into piles, and these two piles are our favorites. "Like/Don't Like" is more organizational than substantive, more automatic than considered, and so shouldn't be given much weight. When someone says, "I like your shoes/your personality/your home/your idea," they're stating an opinion. Opinions are, more often than not, self-defining. They're meant to reveal something about the speaker's preferences. It's the same when I say I like or don't like your work: I'm not telling you anything about your writing; I'm telling you about *my* tastes, values, and sensibilities. If the opinion comes from someone famous or revered, we give it even more weight, but in fact, it's still just a reflection of the person offering the opinion. There's no reason to reject or accept an opinion. Just let it ride.

Idle or unconsidered comments

Sometimes people don't know how to express their feelings in a productive way, but they still feel the need to express *something.* Unlike with opinions, your gut feeling about feedback can be employed here. If you feel real encouragement, as in, the comment makes you feel courageous, then there's probably something useful in it. Let it in and work with it. If you receive a comment that makes you feel diminished, as with a confusing comparison of your work to another artist's, feel free to dismiss it. Trust that feeling. A comment is only useful if it helps you make your work better—see the next section for more on this.

Personally motivated comments

Many people view art through the lens of their emotions, beliefs, ethics, issues, or physical discomfort. They might be speaking out of their personal dislike for the characters, setting, or theme of your work. They might be motivated by a desire to display their intellect, impress you, or raise their status. This is very human, but it's the least helpful sort of feedback because rather than consider your work, it uses your work as a platform, scapegoat, or release valve. It's most likely got some toxic junk tied up in it. You don't need anyone's toxic junk anywhere near your creativity, so even if there's something useful in there, it's not worth it to try and dig it out. Let it go.

Considered, compassionate, and conscious feedback

Bingo! Here is the only feedback that can be counted on to make a real difference. It can reveal something useful about your work, something you might not have been able to see on your own, and here's the most important thing—it leaves you excited to get back to your work, rather than turning you off to it. (More about what this feedback is and where to get it in Practice #33.)

Very few people have mastered the art of giving feedback in a way that's helpful to the work. The art of constructive criticism is not a part of our standard education. Even in graduate-level critique groups, it's often a free-for-all in which rules, goals, or ethics are not discussed beforehand. The fact is, unthoughtful, unskilled, unguided feedback can be terribly damaging. I know this because most every artist I've met is working around some old wound from a remark that cut too deep. In most cases, the person who made the remark had no idea of the damage it caused, but was just flinging their thoughts and opinions around like a novice ninja with a new set of nunchakus.

So train your ears to parse the feedback you receive by considering the source and the agenda. Rather than focusing on whether it's positive or negative, decide if it's useful or not useful. Whether it comes from an expert or amateur, decide whether it's carefully considered or self-serving. Developing this kind of discernment, this kind of "listening," will make you a better writer.

Prompt: Hearing Test

Step One: "Compliments, Praise, Prizes, or Awards." List any compliments, praise, prizes, or awards you've received. In case your mind is freezing up, compliments sound like this: *Beautiful poem. You're the best, Mom! You grew this tomato?! I want you on my team.* Prizes and awards include things like winning a race, getting a promotion, landing a grant, being voted head of the PTA, or winning best costume. List for six minutes.

Note: I wouldn't normally encourage you to censor your pen, but in this case, please avoid backhanded or false compliments: "You look great for your age," or "You're so brave to ask for that promotion with your limited experience!" That's just your inner critic sneaking up on you through your pen.

Step Two: Rate for encouragement. Go through the list you created in step one and put a star by any of the items that make you feel genuinely encouraged, and so braver. Next, put a circle by any compliments that say more about the speaker than you or your work. Some may have both a circle and a star. Some may have neither. Lastly, underline anything that really annoyed your inner critic. Always notice what pisses him off so you can do more of it.

Practice #33: Cull and Cultivate

What are the hallmarks of considered and conscious feedback?

In my writing groups, the question that guides our feedback

is: "Does it help the writing become what it *wants* to become, or what you *think* it should become?" This evolved because my own early experiences with feedback were confusing, with many people telling me what was wrong with my story without first identifying what I was striving for. Good feedback takes the author's intentions into account or helps the author clarify her intentions, then looks at whether those intentions are being fulfilled in the execution.

The second rule is "Consider the stage of development." For instance, imagine you have a four-year-old child and you want her to grow up to be the best person she can be. Do you put her in front of a group of impartial judges and ask them all to say what's wrong with her? "Well, her eyes are pretty close together, and she has that thin hair that's so hard to style. What're you studying, honey? Music and coloring? Let's see one of your drawings. Yikes; well, you're no Michelangelo. Let's hear you sing a little something." Rather than a strong start, this is a good method for launching a child—or a fledgling story—on a confused and neurotic journey.

Early on, your project needs you to watch it for clues as to what it's trying to become. Later on, it will need more structure and discipline. Anyone that you involve in your process should understand this as well. A great question to pose before giving feedback is, "Where are you in the process, and what kind of feedback are you looking for?" If no one asks you, don't hesitate to volunteer the information: "This is fairly raw; I don't know what it is yet." Or "I've overworked this and lost perspective."

The third and most important rule is "Keep the writer writing." This is vitally important because egos definitely influence mouths and sometimes they outright run them. Grace and goodwill should play a big part in the giving of feedback, or else egos will assert themselves. If you listen, you can tell when someone is showing off or grandstanding. Keep your work away from such people. Even if what they say is true, when the truth is delivered in a spray of shrapnel, you'll be too shredded to make the best use of it. No motivation comes from discouragement: if someone is using your work as a platform to showcase their snarky smartness or big vocabulary or literary chops, they don't have your work's best interests at heart. Period.

It's possible to give astute criticism while also fostering the writer's will to work. This is the skill you want to look for in others and develop in yourself. Until I've taken a project as far as I can, I share it only with a carefully culled group of people who have intimate knowledge of the creative process, take me seriously, and champion my intentions. I listen to them because they know me and my work and can help me see when I'm on or off track. This gives me courage because their perspective covers my blind spots and I know they won't let me send my work out undercooked. As a result, I can explore, take risks, and let my writing find its way.

The only reason to reach out for feedback is to help the work reach its greatest potential, not to show how tough-skinned you can be. The goal of receiving feedback is to empower yourself as a writer. You want to learn to take in the remarks that will eliminate your blind spots, fire your drive, and help you improve your craft.

Cull and cultivate
your feedback crew.

IV

Vive La Resistance!

Bring On the Revolution!

If you unfriend all your inner critics, how will you know whether you're doing your best work and reaching your highest potential? There are deeper, more powerful, and more stable inner resources that you can tap and trust to let you know when you're moving in the right direction.

19

Vulnerability—Burning Brighter

Play with Fire / Attend to the Coals

One of the most nakedly vulnerable experiences a human being can have is that of rehearsing for a play. You're in a room full of people who are watching your every move. Some are rooting for you. Some are judging you, certain you only got the role because you knew the writer. You're diving in and out of extreme emotional states and wrestling with hairpieces and corsets and kissing people you barely know who smell unfamiliar and feel weird in your arms, and your attempt at the dialect just sounds like a severe speech impediment. You're bound to feel foolish much of the time, but if you let self-consciousness get hold of you, it will freeze you right out of your creative instincts, and then you'll really be in trouble.

A director can make all the difference in this regard, and in my experience, there are two kinds.

The first kind of director grabs his hair with both hands because you're making his head explode. He can be found brooding and pacing at the back of the room, getting distance from the appalling work you're doing. He snaps at you when you forget to pick up the spoon on the right beat. Your body feels conspicuously large and your brain isn't firing right. The harder you try, the more self-conscious you get. The more self-conscious you get, the harder you try.

The second kind of director says, "Let's stumble through and see what happens."

He's really quiet out there, so you sneak a glance. In the glow from the stage manager's lamp you can see his face, eyes wide, jaw slack, slight smile. You must be doing okay. Then you forget anybody's watching and find your groove.

When you get caught up in a moment and space your line, he says, "Oooh, what was happening for you there?"

Oh, shit. And things were going so well. There's no good answer, so you just admit, "I was thinking I wanted to touch her hand, and then I forgot—"

He lights up. "Oh, my God! Do that! Take it back a couple of lines and touch her hand there!"

And a big discovery is made because it was a great impulse. Or it wasn't a great impulse, but the invitation to pay attention to impulses lets you off the leash. Now you're taking risks, and instead of being afraid of mistakes you're turning them into discoveries.

Guess which kind of director I prefer.

Practice #34: Play with Fire

The conventional wisdom is that the harder we whip ourselves and each other, the better we'll do. The more impossible our standards, the more we yank on our bootstraps, the sterner, the stricter, the tougher we are, the more we think we'll achieve. Well, yanking on bootstraps may be the best way to survive a Siberian winter, but it's not so good for creativity.

You do your best creative work when you're vulnerable and your heart is open. When you're vulnerable, your normally vigilant ego flops onto its back for a tummy rub. Vulnerability is not passive or weak, mind you. Nor is it reckless. It's a state of conscious and tremulous trust, a state in which great things are possible. Yes, unguarded as you are, there's the risk of rejection and embarrassment. But there's also the possibility for discovery and connection and leaps of understanding. The possibilities are absolutely worth the risks.

The problem is that vulnerability can easily tip over into self-consciousness. In an environment that's hostile to vulnerability, the heart armors up, hunkers down, and puts the ego on high alert.

An environment that is hostile to vulnerability is one in which a lack of vigilance on your part could result in being yelled at, scorned, or dismissed. Sharing the best parts of yourself—your curiosity, your empathy, your tenderness, your eager spirit—might expose you to real peril. If you share your light, it may be blown out.

But you can't count on conditions to always be favorable. No matter how you contrive to avoid them, there are folks who just blow out any flame that comes into range. Sometimes we even smother our own flame if it draws the wrong kind of attention. The problem is that once it's out, it's not easily relit.

Take my dog, Al, for instance. Al never needed a leash. We walked everywhere in town and in the wilderness and I never worried about her because if I called, she came, 100 percent of the time. What I didn't account for is that other people didn't have this same deal with their off-leash dogs. One day, Al and I were tramping around in one of Ojai's pretty little meadows when a very large white blur came hurtling at us, its owner calling frantically, to no avail. Al wasn't too hurt, but the white dog did pull out a mouthful of her fur before he turned and trotted away with maddening cool, leaving us in trembling ruins.

The next time I walked Al, she didn't wait for any dogs to jump her—she bared her teeth at first look. If the dog continued to approach, she'd give a warning snap, and if he kept coming and got in her face, she'd lay a neat red stripe across his nose with the business end of her eyetooth and send him yipping away.

"Al! No, no, no!"

I told her what a bad strategy this was, how aggression provokes aggression, but she was taking no chances. She no longer trusted me to keep us safe.

I had to work hard to get her back to her old at-ease off-leash self. I carried a squirt bottle and blasted any dog that ignored my commands to stay back. This earned me dirty looks and curses from dog owners, but you gotta do what you gotta do. I adopted an arms-akimbo, wide-legged stance and deep commanding voice to show Al that I had things well in hand. In time, our walks stopped being white-knuckle search-and-destroy missions, and she relaxed into sniffing and frisking.

Protection smothers vulnerability.

It takes just one surprise attack to get your guard up, and it can be murder getting it back down. So how do you protect your flame without smothering it or baring your teeth?

Well, that's the tricky thing. I don't think you can. Protection is antithetical to vulnerability. It's reasonable to carry a spray bottle when your vulnerability is recovering from a trauma. You must take time to regain your footing. But you can't make a life practice of snapping at or power spraying everything that comes near your underbelly and still expect your vulnerability to get stronger. The goal was not to give Al a dog-free world, but to get her to relax again in the presence of other dogs.

When you're ready, and only when you're ready, you can move on from protecting your flame to tending and building it until it's so strong it can't be blown out. I'm talking about strengthening your essential, playful, engaged you-ness. I'm talking about learning to burn bright, even when conditions are less than ideal.

Practice #35: Attend to the Coals

There are two important steps to building a good, hot fire: fueling and fanning. But in the end, it's all about having a good foundation of coals. If your coals are hot enough, you can toss a damp, green log on there and, with a little fanning, it'll light right up.

First, you need proper fuel. I'm a big believer in good kindling and lots of it. My favorite kindling is a certain kind of pinecone, and I go on regular gathering excursions so that I have enough for the winter.

Your creative kindling is anybody or anything that makes you burn brighter. Notice when you feel brave and awake and easy in your body, when you're being fully yourself and liking it. Then notice who and what is around you. *Really* notice, because if it's good fuel, you want to stack it up in your life. Whether it's a person or group of people, an activity, an object, a poet, a book, or a song, if it stokes you, get more of it.

I have to be honest: fueling doesn't come naturally to me. I had to really work at it. For instance, rather than choose relationships that fed me, I was attracted to the ones that were hard on me. I guess the idea was that if anyone loved me just the way I was, I would get lazy and stop working on myself. So I had to be hit with a wrecking ball of unconditional love before I really saw its value. That wrecking ball came in the form of my husband. I almost rejected him on the basis of this one quality—the way he gazed at me with naked appreciation. When we met, I was standing by my truck behind the theater, having just stopped by to meet a student. He was outside building a set, looking pretty manly in his tool belt. We exchanged pleasantries, and when I got home I saw that I was sweat-streaked and covered with dirt from a rambunctious hike with Al and had hat hair. Why had he been looking at me with such interest?

Much later, he told me that the mud pegged me as adventurous and nature loving, the dog said I was responsible and compassionate, and my truck had a manual transmission, which apparently meant I was capable. All this added up to something irresistible to him. I remember wondering if he was simple or something. Or nearsighted. He definitely wasn't rigorous enough in his standards. But that's the thing about a wrecking ball: it won't be denied. He busted through my defenses and relationship doctrine, and his genuine appreciation lit me up. I burned brighter. I got braver. It was a real consciousness jump for me.

It's counterintuitive to starve a fire that's meant to warm you, but that's what I had been doing. If you're doing that, cut it out. Fuel. Feed. Kindle.

Once you've got a nice little blaze going, you can start with the fanning. This means you strategically expose your flame to a nice stiff breeze. For instance, you might act on a strong impulse to hug someone rather than playing it safe and just patting them on the shoulder. You might trust someone with a secret or ask for forgiveness from an estranged friend. If you're burning really bright, you could take an improv class or go all out on karaoke night. Do something you aren't good at. Talk to someone who scares you. Ask for something from someone who's as likely as not to turn you down. Take a little risk, act on an impulse, open your heart, share.

When you execute one of these fanning missions, it's not enough to just survive it. You must *notice* that you survived it. Whether or not you deem the mission a success doesn't really matter. For instance, say you ask someone on a date. Regardless of their response, what matters is that you ventured something and survived. Each time you do this, *notice* that you survived and celebrate your wild bravery. Notice how alive you feel as a result of getting through that event in one piece. It's the venturing that's badass, no matter what the outcome. Start small, with missions you are absolutely sure you can ace, and get more daring as you feel stronger. And remember, we're going for more resilient vulnerability, not a thicker skin.

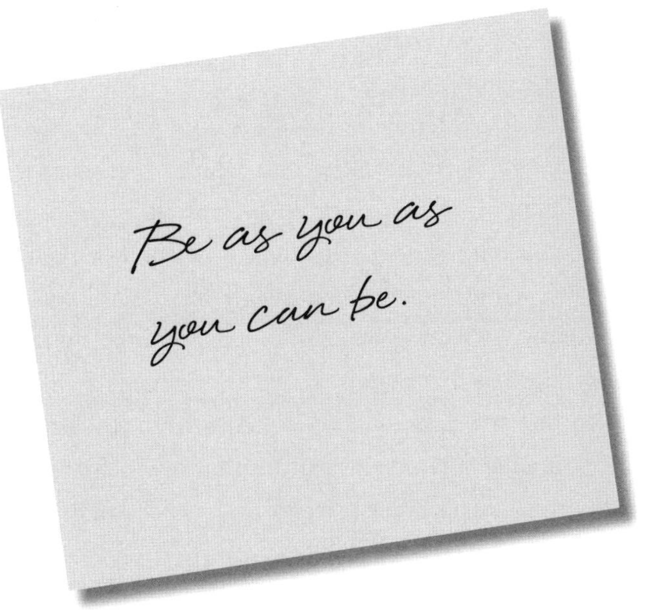

You're not inviting all this nice inspiring stuff into your life in order to insulate yourself and get comfy and fall asleep. That's not why you're reading this book. That's not who you are.

Think of your inner fire searing away anything that's been hiding or diluting *you*: your spirit, your ideas, your story, your wildness, all the things that make you unique. That's what you want to strengthen and share. That's what you create from. The more *you* you are, the brighter you burn, the better your work will be.

Prompt: Fueling and Fanning

Step One: List what makes you burn brighter. List anything that makes you feel inspired, uplifted, brighter, sexier, or more expansive: *a perfectly ripe fig right off the tree*; *slanting afternoon light, especially if it's slanting through eucalyptus trees*; *awkward bravery*; *muscle soreness*; *my dog's welcome-home dance*; *dunking my head in a cold lake*. Does it make you curious, lighter, joyful, determined? Does it make you want to write? Put it on the list. No descriptions necessary, just list for six minutes.

Step Two: Mine your list. Read back through the list and notice how it makes you feel. Underline or highlight anything that is especially potent or positive. If you think of more things that make you burn bright, put them on the list now. Were there things on the list that you really enjoy, but no longer find time for? Put a star by those and see if you can work them back into your life, even if only in small doses. Keep this list handy and add to it every time you think of or notice anything else that makes you burn brighter.

Step Three: Map your fire. Choose an item from the list that really heats you up and let it bloom in your mind, whether it's being held in someone's arms, stepping into a hot bath, or watching your children sleep. Notice what's going on in your body as you indulge this fantasy. Where do you feel the lift, the warmth? Maybe you're smiling. Maybe you feel a tingle. Put your hand on the spot where you feel this experience in your body. Open your eyes and draw the feeling on your body map (see p. 223) or just circle the area(s) where the feeling occurs.

Step Four: Fan your fire. Finish the sentence "I'm wary of . . ." and see where it takes you. *I'm wary of cats, costume parties, prolonged eye contact, men who jingle their change*; *I'm wary of too-good-looking people*; *I'm wary of asking for help.* Don't feel like you have to discover anything profound or even useful. Just give it a go. Write for six minutes.

You can also try:

* I'm shy around . . .
* I'm afraid of . . .
* I'm uncomfortable with . . .
* I'm saying no to . . .

Read back over your writing and underline something that you feel you could safely take on. For instance, you could handle asking someone to hold eye contact with you for sixty seconds, or you could ask your coworker to take over some of your accounts. Make sure it's something that will give you a stretch, but not something that will tear a muscle. Do it. Survive it. Notice that you survived it. Take a week off. Do another one.

Bonus Prompts: Fire Extinguishers

Make a list of things that douse or dampen you. You can't get rid of them if you're not aware of them.

Make a list of people who starve your fire of oxygen. Underline the ones you can break up with or let go of.

Make a list of activities and substances that you use, to any degree, to numb your emotions or nerves—anything from cat videos to narcotics. Don't beat yourself up about them; just bring them to awareness.

20

The Champion—Being Held

Use Your Powers for Good / Meet Your Greatest Resource / Hand Over the Reins

When I was twenty-eight, I had my one and only metaphysical experience.

I had given up on acting, but I was still afraid of writing. I was not getting married to Greg after all. I was still living in Brooklyn and working in the city and had no idea what I was even doing on the East Coast. I had lost all sense of my life's direction and meaning. I was coming apart. And I was quitting smoking for the five hundredth—and, I hoped, last—time. Oh, my God, the smoking. I went to several Nicotine Anonymous meetings a week and took life one minute at a time.

One thing I had going for me was a little studio apartment I'd found in a dangerous neighborhood right next to a safe neighborhood right next to Prospect Park, which I loved more than Central Park, more than Golden Gate Park, more than any park I'd ever loved before. I went running there every other day and came home to my little studio, which was quiet because it was in the back of the building. It had three tall windows, and the one at the head of my bed opened onto a giant blooming catalpa tree.

As much of a refuge as my studio was, there was one particular night when it became the most lonely place on earth. I had gone to see a movie. I don't remember what it was—some police drama. It didn't matter. There was something about going to movies by myself that was saving my life at the time. It was the only place I could really rest. But this movie had a shoot-out scene that went on for the longest time, and the longer it went on, the more riled the audience got. Now, I was in Brooklyn, where audiences of any kind tended to be more vocal, but this was not that. They were *cheering.* They were cheering the body count—cops, bad guys, bystanders—with what could only be called bloodlust. My existential anxiety needle went into the red, and I began to shake. My tenuous grip on life's meaning slipped. What meaning could life have when this is what stories were doing in the world?

I ran out of the movie theater and dashed the few blocks home, unlocked all the locks, locked all the locks again, and threw myself into my one chair. I had been avoiding the whole Higher Power thing they were pushing at Nic Anon, but now I prayed. I prayed to just feel something greater than myself, something to tether myself to so that I didn't sink.

And there was nothing. An obstinate, endless silence.

I cried and shook and gritted my teeth and somehow I managed not to smoke.

I woke up in my bed. The catalpa tree was there; I had half expected it to be gone. And that's when the metaphysical thing happened. There was somebody there with me, behind me, holding me. There really was, even though there wasn't. I felt a strong, compact body pressed up against mine. My brain struggled against the impossibility for a minute, and then it stopped struggling altogether. I was safe. I knew the value of life. I knew I was okay. I knew I would quit smoking.

It started happening a lot. I might be staring into the fridge, hanging from the subway bar, or lying in bed, and he'd appear, wrapping me in a protective embrace. I called him the Spirit Guy, and he gave me several months of spontaneous, loving, platonic refuge. In that time, I stopped being afraid. I went from not knowing anything to knowing one thing very clearly: I was ready to write.

I called my friend Nancy and told her if she still wanted to write with me, I was ready. Soon we had a writing group, and not long after that, I moved back to California and eventually wrote my first play.

The Spirit Guy disappeared. One day he was just gone. But I was changed. He left me with a sense of myself as resourceful and renewable. He reminded me I didn't have to be afraid.

Years later, I told my husband about this experience, and he showed me an article from a medical journal that described my experience precisely—the feeling of being held or cradled—and explained how it could be induced by certain stressors or by stimulating a certain area of the brain. At first I was deflated. I didn't want my Spirit Guy to be a brain tic.

But then I thought, *Well, of course.* Why wouldn't our brains be equipped to provide us with exactly the support and guidance we need? Whether the Spirit Guy stepped through a metaphysical portal or bloomed from within my own brain or was triggered in my brain by a metaphysical force—who cares? When I was utterly lost and my fire had gone cold and I needed rescue, he came along with tinder and a compass.

Practice #36: Use Your Powers for Good

When I bring up the idea of the inner champion in a workshop, the initial response is a mass eye roll. *Oh, here we go; she's going to get out the candles and rain sticks and it's gonna be all goddess power and spirit animals and surrounding my creativity with white light.*

Hey, I get it. Most people are wary about calling on support, even—or maybe especially—when that support is coming from inside them. It's the believe-in-yourself stuff of motivational posters.

I will point out, though, that I get no such reaction when I bring up the topic of inner critics. Instead of eyes rolling, it's heads nodding. How is it that we readily believe in the inner critic while scoffing at the mere notion of an inner champion? Yes, isn't that interesting! Then there's the Muse, the Source, the Flow—all these merit suspending our disbelief. But an *internal* power source? That's just silly.

What do creative people do? We become curious about a thought or an idea or a character or an image, and we invest and investigate and it comes a little bit to life and then we pursue it with some real energy and it becomes dimensional and real, not just for us but for others as well. Creative people make thoughts, which have no substance, into songs, stories, software, buildings, social movements—things that exist in the real world and can affect the people who interact with them. That's the creative person's superpower, *your* superpower. Turning nothing into something through the miracle of imagination and belief.

But—and this is a big *but*, this is the *but* that this whole book is born from—if not used consciously, your superpower can work against you when you believe in the thoughts that hinder and not the ones that help.

The brain's default M.O. is to scan for trouble. *Is a saber-toothed tiger going to jump out from behind that bush? Is a child going to jump in front of my car? Anything could happen, so scan, scan, scan.* If your brain can't find any present danger, it'll look for probable danger. What if you run out of money? What if your wife loses interest in you? Our ability to believe and feel what we imagine can be used both for creating and for killing creativity.

If I tell you there's a nest of vipers under your desk, you'll immediately see it in your mind's eye: scales, flickering tongues, slithering, hissing. It's there, physical and fully formed, creeping you out, making your shins feel exposed. If I tell you there are no snakes after all, but there is a basket of puppies under there, you'll practically feel the fur and smell the puppy breath, and instead of shrinking back from your desk you'll be tempted to peek under it, half hoping to see some adorable baby beagles. But there are no snakes, and no puppies, except the ones that you made with your thoughts.

So here's the thing you need to know to gain real creative purchase: just as your imaginative powers can make you believe what the nest of hissing critics in your head say, they can also give a voice of loving, active support to your inner champion.

Remember: invest consciously and wisely. Invest heavily in the thoughts that serve your creative efforts.

Practice #37: Meet Your Greatest Resource

Like the Spirit Guy, the inner champion has your back. I call her the champion because mine champions my cause. She is my Olympian, Amazonian flame bearer, and she can run for a hundred miles and never let that flame go out. I call her *her* because mine is female. Yours may be an inner lion or an inner Wise One. They come in a wide array of personalities, species, forms, and genders.

Your champion knows your worst fears and can hold you together while you face and overcome them. She knows what you're capable of, the depth of your resources, and who you are at your very core. She knows why you *must* create, and if you let her, she'll bring all her power and wisdom to the service of your creative process. The champion can see, with crystal clarity, the particular power that your voice carries. She can help you more than any book, teacher, or mentor.

Your champion has been trying to make contact. This is the voice that keeps calling you back to the page because you have a story to tell. Your champion is quivering with anticipation. She can't wait for you to write the next word, and the next.

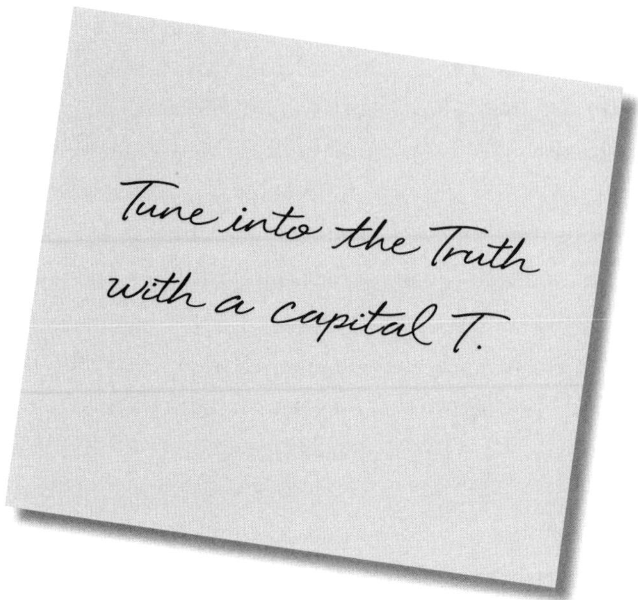
Tune into the Truth
with a capital T.

Maybe it's unnerving or even dangerous to listen to this voice, to be encouraged in your writing. What if you let yourself believe that your creativity, your writing, matters? The inner champion knows that failure is a possibility, and she is your best resource for learning how to transcend failure and keep working. Your inner champion believes wholeheartedly that what's most important is the process of writing, because when we're writing, we are becoming.

Know, too, that the inner champion is yours for life. She has chosen you and has devoted herself to you. All that she has, which is a lot, is yours. All you have to do is ask.

Tune into that still, small voice that knows the Truth with a capital T—the voice that knows you were born to create. This is the smartest, oldest, wisest part of you. You'll recognize the voice by its fierce, unguarded love, its limitless strength, its robust permission and invitation. You'll know it by the way it makes you brave when you tune it in and turn up the volume.

Prompt: Make Contact

Step One: Map your champ. Turn toward the part of you that wants to write and create. Where does that restive energy reside in your body and inner landscape? You might feel it as a lift, a charge, a muscularity, a stillness, a flame, a playfulness. Perhaps there is a part of your body where you tend to hold or hide things; that's a good place to look. Put your hand on the part of your body where you feel the champion's energy the most. What comes up—images, sensations, memories, colors, words? Put that feeling or force on the body map (see p. 223).

Step Two: "Everything I Know about My Inner Champion." Reach for any details about or clues to your champion's nature. Is it young? Old? Ancient? Is it human? Does it have a gender? A shape? How do you relate to it? How do you experience it? What characteristics does it have? Is it associated with a color? A place? An element? Just be curious. Be a detective. In my workshops, inner champions have appeared as coyotes, fire keepers, mists, departed loved ones, and dragons. One young man had a Cookie Monster–type creature that was huuuungry for his writing. Someone else's inner champion had been calling for years, hoping he'd pick up. There may be more than one inner champion. One writer had a council of four, always mounted on horseback. Who are we to question? Just reach out. It's all right if you feel like you're making it up. Just write what comes for six minutes.

Practice #38: Hand Over the Reins

One of the most thrilling and gratifying things about running a theater was that my job was basically to champion artists. Raising money really rubbed my fur the wrong way, but I did it anyway because as long as we kept the lights on, I got to give plays their first productions and help people write their first plays. All my Holy-Roller, unleash-the-creativity-and-save-the-world energy had a full-time occupation.

Fiercely, feverishly I took groups of writers, seven or eight at a time, through the process of writing a play and having it read publicly by professional actors. Each time we did it, I saw people go from shaking in their boots to shining from the inside as a result of telling and sharing a story. I had writing groups and workshops and readings and showcases and new-work festivals. I was saving the world one released writer at a time and I was not kidding around. I was a true believer.

Meanwhile, I wasn't writing at all. My creativity tried to push up through the cracks for the first year or two, and then it went underground. If anyone needed a writing champion, I was the girl for the job. But if my own inner champion tried to put a pen in my hand, likely as not I'd have poked her in the eye with it. *No time! Not now!*

A lot of artists live with this cognitive dissonance: *Art is desperately important/My art can wait.*

After the theater closed and things quieted down a bit, my inner champion finally reappeared and spoke up. "We're moving to the woods." She wasn't asking. She was telling.

What woods? Where?

"Don't you worry about that. Go get some sleep and then start packing." Luckily, Chris liked the idea.

She's been holding the reins ever since, and it's such a relief. I know I should be able to champion my own art, walk my talk. But as long as I'm in charge, there's going to be the possibility of derailment. Just like my students did, I need someone to tell me, with quiet vehemence, to stop arguing and make my art. I needed a higher authority. I needed, frankly, a rescue.

Put your inner
champion in charge.

Make contact with your inner champion, allow yourself to believe in her, let yourself be rescued, and then hand over the reins.

The inner champion can be especially helpful at the beginning of the writing process, creating a safe place, defending you against interruptions, fostering your vulnerability and curiosity, encouraging risk, letting you know when you're "on voice," etc. Later, in the rewrite stage, she can be counted on to provide a discerning eye, to help you cut away the fat and find mistakes. The inner champion not only knows what's best for you, she knows when you're doing your best work because her vision isn't clouded by fear. She knows when you need to dig deeper and also when you need to lighten up.

Once you've made contact with your inner champion, you will no longer have any need to look to an inner critic for guidance. You will have taken the expert status away from your inner critic and assigned it to its rightful owner, your inner champion. But this transfer of power isn't always easy or smooth: notice your reluctance to let go of the demeaning, whip-cracking inner critic in favor of a dependable, *devoted* inner champion. Then do it anyway. You can have no doubt about which one is going to engage you in the more productive relationship.

Task your inner champion with firing your inner critic or reassigning it to nonessential tasks. Filing, maybe?

Park your inner champion in the chair next to your desk. Put it in your pocket before you leave the house each morning. Draw wisdom and courage from this endless resource. Put your inner champion in charge—of you, of your writing, of your inner critic, of the whole operation. The inner champion is passionate enough to ensure that everybody—including you—is serving the writing with integrity.

Prompt: Believe

Step One: Interview your inner champion. Draw your inner champion toward you and listen. Ask it what it would like to say to you. Write down the answer you receive. Write in first person, from the inner champion's point of view: *"Hi, I'm so glad to hear from you!"* Let it tell you all the things it's been dying to say. The voice might be weak and faint at first. It might feel like you're reaching, but keep going. If this relationship is new, you need to go easy and keep your expectations in check. When your inner champion first speaks up, it might feel phony or stilted. No matter. Listen closely. Take dictation as your inner champion speaks to any of the following topics:

1. Why it chose you.
2. Why you must answer the call to create.
3. How it can help you create.

Write for six minutes or more.

Note: Your inner critic might pipe up during this exercise. Pin it to the page and keep moving. Don't ignore it or allow it to hitch a ride on your inner champion's goodwill with twisted "support" such as, "Hey, just because you're not good at anything else doesn't mean you aren't good at writing." The inner critic won't like that you're invoking a more empathic, empowering source. It'll want you to feel embarrassed. It'll accuse you of making it up, of being Pollyanna, of being self-indulgent. Your inner critic will say you've lost the connection, or that you should wait till you "feel" it, or even that you're too broken to have an inner champion at all. But it's just playing on your fears to delay creating any way it can. Like any tyrannical regime, its goal is self-perpetuation, and it rightly senses that the inner champion is a real threat.

Step Two: Commit to your inner champion. This is just the first step. You may not be able to make a solid connection with your inner champion after just half an hour of investment and inquiry. Hold the image that is forming up and allow your inner champion to continue to manifest. Don't try. Don't push. Just allow, be curious, and keep reaching out.

First and Last

First and last, forgive yourself for not starting soon enough, not finishing soon enough, not being enough.

Forgive yourself for not being the wunderkind they all said you would be, for not "making it" before you were thirty.

Or fifty.

Or seventy.

Forgive yourself for being too afraid to write that second book, for stalling, for hiding.

Forgive yourself for not finishing your thesis or getting your degree.

Forgive yourself for not being brave, for not fighting for your space and your voice and your right to create.

Forgive yourself for not being able to write the poem or the story as well as you felt it in your bones and saw it in your mind's eye.

Forgive yourself for not understanding what your book was about until after it was written.

Forgive your big, embarrassing failures and the private, secret failures, too.

Forgive yourself for caring for everyone and everything before caring for your creativity.

Forgive yourself for being fragile.

Forgive yourself for not yet forgiving yourself.

Forgive yourself for not starting and start.

Forgive yourself for not writing perfectly and strive to write well.

It's not too late. It's never too late. Start now. Write and let each word be a benediction, releasing you from the tyranny of your not-enoughness. Know that writing is the great redeemer. Grief and joy, sin and virtue, failure and triumph—art can bear the weight of anything human. Not only that, it can transform it. Writing is both the reason you must forgive yourself and the absolution you seek.

Whatever it is that needs forgiving, you've paid for it already. You've paid with pain and with separateness. Whatever burden remains, give it to the writing.

Start now. Start again. Start every day.

Serve writing, practice writing, offer yourself up to writing and let it save you, page by page.

The Part Wild Guide to Writing in Packs

Some of you might enjoy doing *Part Wild* prompts in groups of two or more. Writing in a pack can:

- add some accountability: people to show up for.
- add some support: people showing up for you.
- provide a regular reminder that you're not the only one struggling with certain aspects of the process.
- form connections that can become sources of support outside the group.

Grab a friend or family member and do some sentence starters. Gather ten people at your local youth or senior center and do some lists and memory-trigger prompts. Do a chapter a week with your writing group. Pull together any people you think might secretly want to write or to revive their writing joy and get your pens moving.

But do it *safely*.

Many of the prompts in *Part Wild* are designed to take the writer into risky and unknown territory. They aim to get at unplanned discovery, and so it's possible for the writing to bring up powerful memories or unexpected emotions. If that's going to happen in the company of others, it's important to have ground rules and protocols that make for a safe, conscientious environment that sincerely champions the creative effort.

Guidelines and protocols are the domain of the tame side of your nature, so here's a great way for it to participate in the creative process by making a safe place for your wild side to get out and play.

I. Environment. A *Part Wild* pack needs the right conditions to thrive.

Space. Ringing phones, rambunctious dogs, a shirtless husband on his way to the garage, cold drafts, or lack of light are the kinds of distractions that can keep a group from really sinking into the process. Try to find or create a focused, well-lit, temperature-controlled environment with comfortable seating that makes writing easy for all—tatami mats and zafu cushions aren't for everyone.

Atmosphere. If you're hosting the pack, you may feel that wine and finger foods will make all feel welcome and relaxed, and you would be right—but it will also make them feel like they're at a party, and once the socializing starts it's hard to turn the tide toward creative work. If your group likes a glass of wine and some social release it's best to save it until after the writing is done. That said, I would never discourage snacks. A bowl of chocolates or nuts will kill the munchies without inciting hobnobbing. Just be sure to choose noiseless snacks that don't have a strong odor so that they don't hijack your writers' senses.

Tone. Writing in a group is reminiscent of school and can trigger either a competitive mind-set or, depending on your disposition, a rebellious one. Head this off by regularly reminding each other that there will be no tests or grades, just judgment-free exploration and play.

Latecomers. It can be very uncomfortable to halt a reader in the middle of a tender revelation while a latecomer fumbles apologetically to a seat. There's no way to ensure 100 percent punctuality, so it's good to have a latecomer policy. For instance: text if you'll be late, knock softly on arrival, and you'll be let in at the next break in the action.

Time. In a group of eight, if all read their writing aloud (and ideally, all will), one prompt will take up to forty-five minutes from start to finish. A three-part prompt can take two or three hours, and so on. Fewer people take less time, obviously, and larger groups take exponentially more. So choose prompts that can be completed comfortably in the time allotted.

Timer. Smartphones make the job easy. Familiarize yourself with your timer app in advance and be sure to pick a ringtone that will gently break the spell rather than jolting the writers back to reality with a blast of sound.

Facilitation. It can be enormously rewarding to be the one to bring creative people together in an environment that fosters and releases their part-wildness. If you have the urge to facilitate a *Part Wild* pack, I invite you to go to my website, partwild.com, and download the *Pack Leader Guide*, which provides more in-depth counsel on forming and running a group.

II. Writing. Writing with others can stir up performance anxiety. Use the following tools and anti-rules to short-circuit those very human but not very creativity-friendly tendencies.

Always, always use the timer.

* The timer reassures you that the exercise will end.
* It keeps you writing past the point of feeling "finished," which can take you into some unexplored terrain.
* It provides a sense of urgency that helps keep your pen moving.
* After a while, the timer's appearance will act as a Pavlovian trigger that primes your best speed-writing brain state.

Speed-writing. It's the core of the practice. Here is a review of how it works:

1. Keep your pen moving. If you write fast enough, self-critical thoughts won't be able to catch you.
2. Don't think. Don't plan. Hopefully you'll stumble onto the surprising thing that you could never get to by grinding your brain's gears.
3. Let go of grammar, spelling, punctuation, or making sense. Laugh when steam comes out of your inner critic's ears.
4. Don't cross anything out or correct anything. A mistake might turn out to be a happy accident.
5. Don't try to be interesting, funny, or brilliant.
6. Lose control.

Say "Yes!" to whatever wants to come out of your pen, regardless of whether you think it will impress the group. Your mind is great at "No!" already, so practice saying "Yes!" Yes is so much more interesting.

Relaxation. Writing in a group may activate the "pushing" instinct. You may find yourself trying to go deeper and stretch further and have a breakthrough in your writing. Exploring your "edge" is encouraged, but this work doesn't benefit from added pressure. Try engaging your boundaries with relaxation, curiosity, and presence and let the prompts do the work for you.

III. Reading. One of the benefits of writing in a pack is that there's a group to read aloud to. Okay, maybe that just gave you a tiny heart attack. Let me tell you why reading aloud is so great and how to make it less heart-attacky.

Confidentiality. Before anyone reads aloud, it is of the utmost importance that everyone in the group take a sacred vow of confidentiality. *Everything* spoken in the writing room must stay in the writing room. This includes not only the writing that is read aloud but also the idlest of comments or jokes made during the break. Knowing that there is a sacred seal of confidentiality allows writers to shed a layer of self-protection or formality and write whatever wants to be written.

Why reading aloud is great. Reading aloud is really all about providing the opportunity to practice listening. As you listen to others, I'll bet you'll feel some genuine curiosity and generosity. You'll wonder about the crazy mixture of genetics and life experiences that it took to create this particular voice. You'll hear the qualities of the writing that make it unique and get excited about the potential in that uniqueness. You'll respect the courage it took for them to write what they wrote. Once you notice this, you can train yourself to listen to your own writing with that same kind of curiosity and empathy. It's true: reading your exercises aloud is a bullet train to humility. So go with it. Be humble before the possibilities and potential in your own writing.

Two reasons not to have a heart attack:

1. As you notice your natural curiosity, generosity, and empathy toward other readers, remember: that's how they're listening when *you* read. Everyone is on your side because they're in your shoes. They're rooting for you and championing your right to explore, risk, and flirt with the edge. Everyone has different challenges and different comfort levels, but everyone is there because of a need to explore. Plant your feet firmly on that common ground and let it stabilize you.
2. Maybe there's something you're just not willing to read aloud. Maybe there's a sentence that is just too exposing, or maybe you wrote about another group member—by all means, redact as you read. You're the boss of what you read aloud. While vulnerability is celebrated, it's not mandated.

Tears and other surprises. You might be surprised by emotion when you read. If a sentence or an image or a revelation brings up tears, it's okay. Don't hide your face or apologize or run from the room. Tears and other strong emotions offer invaluable information. They tell you when something is stirring in your writing and where to dig.

My husband is a tender soul and cries easily. Early in our relationship, he was embarrassed about this, but now we call it his "mist-o-meter." Whenever the mist-o-meter goes off it means the writing is hitting on a human level, and that's great information.

If tears arise, stay seated and keep reading. It's all right if your voice gets squeaky and you cry-grimace. There are no extra points for poise or prettiness in this process. Let it ride.

IV. Listening. We tend to listen to new writing with an analytical ear. In a *Part Wild* pack, we do it differently.

Listening practice. As your packmates read, drop down out of your intellect, out of your judging and comparing mind, and land in your body. Root yourself there. Listen with your whole physical-sensory-visual-emotional self and notice how you're reacting, *viscerally*, to what you're hearing. Do you get a chill or a flash of anger? Do you well up, smell motor oil, see a clear image of your grandfather's hands? Really work this practice so that you can listen to your own writing this way. "How does the writing affect me?" is a much more interesting question than "Do I like the writing?" or "Is the writing any good?" Notice when your "thinky" mind tries to get involved, how badly it wants to diagnose and fix, then scooch farther down into your body to retrieve a more valuable kind of information.

Holding the space. Aside from the information they offer about the writing, tears soften the hearts of all present. Softening and opening are good for writing. For this reason, if a reader is surprised by emotion, an atmosphere of empathy and support is all that is required. You needn't hug or soothe or fix them in any way. Just hand them a tissue and encourage them to keep reading.

V. Responding. Whenever human beings read aloud in a group, there will be the impulse to respond. At this early stage of creating, the responding needs to be very conscious.

Don't respond with critical feedback. This work is not ready for critique. It's just been dragged straight from your guts, your mental storage room, or your unconscious mind. First it needs to just be heard. Later you might reflect on it or interpret it. Somewhere down the line you might develop it into something that will benefit from feedback. But not yet.

Don't respond with advice. It's likely that some intriguing revelations will escape onto the page, and these will ignite all kinds of curiosity and empathy and a desire to reach out in a personal way. If someone writes about a car crash, you want to know how the survivors are doing. If they write about addiction, you want to recommend your favorite twelve-step group. If they write about a loss, you want to share your own experience with grief. Unfortunately, this can cause self-consciousness because it holds the writer accountable for a mess of words that just flew, uncensored, onto a page. They may be a complete mystery to the writer. They may be too difficult to talk about. They may not even be true. It's one thing to evacuate a thought onto a page, it's another thing entirely to have a discussion about it. Avoid "cross-talk" and you'll avoid the self-censoring that results from it.

Do respond with repetition. When the reader finishes, repeat back any words or phrases that affected you. By "affected you," I mean that as you listened from a visceral and emotional place, you noticed a tightening in your muscles, a prickle of fear or longing, anything at all. Don't share the reaction. Just share the words or phrases that prompted it. It's very important that you just repeat, without added commentary.

Here's why: whether positive or negative, at this stage, specific feedback of any kind can take a writer away from his instincts. It's just the way humans are built: whatever is praised we do more of, and whatever isn't praised we do less of. What you want from *Part Wild* prompts is a strengthening of intuition and voice, and this won't happen if you're writing to please the pack.

So it will feel weird at first, but don't attach any qualifier, opinion, or explanation to your repetition. No "It was so evocative." No "You really must develop this!" Simple repetition gives you a way to respond, honor your reactions, acknowledge what's got power, and avoid not only the foibles of premature feedback but also the awkwardness of silence.

I find repeating works best when you don't take turns, but just call the words and phrases out. If several people offer the same repetitions, a "Me, too" is fine.

There will always be someone who spaced out, people with great short-term memories and people with terrible ones. Don't get too hung up on getting it right. Don't worry if you can't remember verbatim. You can say, "I heard something about an orange cloud toward the end."

Keep it playful. It's something that you get better at with practice.

Underlining. As the writer who is receiving these repetitions, your job is to underline. When someone says, "I heard 'the river was too swift,'" find it in your writing and underline it. Hopefully they'll be coming at you a little too fast. Probably you'll have a hard time finding them, or won't be able to read your writing. It's okay. Just do your best. It's all right if you miss some. The main thing is to honor your groupmates for listening and get a sense of what is resonating for others in your writing—for *whatever* reason.

Be kind. Be outrageous. Be messy. Champion the writing of your pack and enjoy a good group howl!

Bonus Prompts

Here are plenty of prompts to ensure that you never have an excuse not to write. Use these:

- to jump-start your writing day.
- when you have a little time to kill in a waiting room.
- to freshen your brain when you're stuck, tired, or in a rut.
- as a daily workout to build muscle, flexibility, and stamina.
- to explore a topic, character, or story.

Remember: Don't try to be brilliant, interesting, or funny. Just write as fast as you can and be curious to see what comes out of your pen.

Memory Triggers

Set the timer for six minutes and write about . . .

a certain someone's perfume or cologne.

a contest.

a difficult decision.

a dirty job you had to do.

a fight that wasn't about what it was about.

a first impression.
a funeral.
a hiding place.
a kindness that mattered.
a long-ago crush.
a pair of shoes that hurt your feet.
a parade.
a promise.
a time someone didn't show up.
a time you faked it.
a time you had to accept help.
a time you held your breath.
a time you overslept.
a time you wanted to leave but stayed.
a time you were claustrophobic.
a time you were doing exactly what you wanted to be doing.
a time you were dressed inappropriately for the occasion.
a time you were suspicious.
a time you were thwarted.
a time you wigged out.
a toy that scared you.
an abandoned building.
an injury.
an object you've had for a long time.
being bitten.
being in a church.
being in a waiting room.
being in or on a boat.
being lied to.
being on an island.
fighting for something.
getting into trouble.

hearing a sound in the distance.
packing or unpacking a box.
sleeping outdoors.
something given to you by a grandparent.
something that happened in a driveway.
something that happened in a hotel or motel.
something that happened on a bus.
something that happened on a deck or a balcony.
something you wanted but couldn't have.
staying over at a friend's house.
staying over at a relative's house.
the morning after.
winning.

How-tos

Set the timer and write the easy-to-follow, step-by-step instructions for . . .

How to Annoy Children
How to Annoy Your Critics
How to Appreciate Beauty
How to Be Born Again
How to Be Happy in Prison
How to Be Humble
How to Behave Badly
How to Bide Time
How to Become Your Mother/Father
How to Be Friends with Your Ex
How to Be Graceful
How to Be Heard
How to Be Normal
How to Be Safe
How to Break Up

How to Build a Fort
How to Capture a Moment
How to Catch a Fairy
How to Change When You Don't Want To
How to Choose a Mate
How to Dance
How to Die Happy
How to Enjoy Chocolate
How to Empty a Nest
How to Enter a Room
How to Forgive Your Parents
How to Get Out of a Rut
How to Get Respect
How to Grow Old Gracefully
How to Judge a Beauty Contest
How to Kiss
How to Listen to a Man
How to Listen to a Woman
How to Live in the Now
How to Make People Like You
How to Make Someone Feel Young
How to Pray
How to Prevent a Fight
How to Read an Aura
How to Rob a Bank
How to Run Amok
How to Sit Still
How to Start a Cult
How to Take Your Writing Seriously
How to Tame a Hummingbird
How to Tread Water
How to Treat Your Housekeeper

How to Win a Hot Dog–eating Contest
How to Win an Argument With a Teenager
How to Write Brilliantly

Launchpads

Set the timer for six minutes and launch from the sentence starter . . .

At night . . .
At the risk of sounding passionate (from *What It Is*, by Lynda Barry) . . .
Before I knew you . . .
Before I was born . . .
Comfort me with . . .
Everything changed when . . .
How come we never . . .
How do you explain . . .
I always meant to . . .
I belong to . . .
I blame . . .
I buried . . .
I can no longer eat . . .
I can tell when you're . . .
I can't live without . . .
I can't remember . . .
I can't stop thinking about . . .
I could never write about . . .
I did not become . . .
I didn't expect . . .
I didn't speak up when . . .
I experimented with . . .
I got away with . . .
I got over . . .

I gotta get me some . . .
I have mastered . . .
I have never been more . . .
I inherited . . .
I keep meaning to . . .
I left . . .
I let . . .
I live for . . .
I loved it when . . .
I lost . . .
I measure time by . . .
I miss . . .
I remember/don't remember . . .
I survived . . .
I stayed . . .
I used to work at . . .
I want to apprentice with . . .
I was not ready . . .
I was scammed by . . .
I was taken apart by . . .
I was taught . . .
I was told never/always to . . .
I was totally myself when . . .
I was wrong about/right about . . .
I wish I were braver about . . .
I wish you were braver about . . .
I woke up this morning . . .
I wonder what ever happened to . . .
If I were king . . .
If I'm honest . . .
If I'm very patient . . .
If only you . . .

If you look closely . . .
I'm dangerous when . . .
I'm fighting to keep from . . .
I'm fueled by . . .
I'm keeping quiet about . . .
I'm optimistic about . . .
I'm plugged into . . .
I'm rethinking . . .
I'm shooting for . . .
I'm shy about . . .
I'm trying not to think about . . .
I'm willing to . . .
In my grandmother's kitchen . . .
In the desert . . .
In your bed . . .
It ain't love if . . .
It's a good thing I didn't . . .
It's poetry when . . .
It was my job to . . .
It was the first time/last time . . .
I used to believe in . . .
Lately I've been noticing . . .
Let us praise . . .
My mother's/father's cooking . . .
Note to self . . .
One day I'm going to surprise you . . .
Other people's families . . .
The last time I saw you . . .
What I really want to say is . . .
When I die . . .
When I look at you, I see . . .
When I'm embarrassed . . .

When I'm in love . . .
When no one is looking . . .
When you look at me . . .
When you're asleep . . .
When you're not around . . .
Why won't you just admit . . .
You promised me . . .
You were instrumental . . .

List Headings

Set the timer for six minutes and make a list of . . .
Backyards I've Known
Beds I've Known
Beginnings
Births/Rebirths/Renewals
Bullies
Cars I've Known
Clothing I've Known
Costumes I've Worn
Crimes I've Committed
Deaths
Distractions
Encounters with Weather
Endings
Family Vacations
Fights
First Times
Gifts Given or Received
Good-byes
Graduations
Happy Times

Heroes
Houseplants I've Known
Jobs I've Done
Kitchens I've Known
Losses
Milestones and Turning Points
Monsters
Motels, Hotels, and Inns I've Known
My Secret Powers
Obsessions
Parties
Peeves
People I Don't Talk to Anymore
People Who Left
People Who Said No to Me
People Who Said Yes to Me
People Who Stayed
People Who've Offered Support
Perfect Moments
Pets I've Known
Pleasures I've Known
Products My Parents Used
Questions
Reasons Not to Quit
Reasons to Write
Roles I Play
Rooms I've Known
Secrets
Shit I Was Right About
Shoes I've Known
Smells That Remind Me of Being a Teenager
Smells That Remind Me of Being in Love

Sounds from Childhood
Sounds I Hear Every Day
Superstitions
Teachers
Temptations
Things I Can't Live Without
Things I Can't Seem to Stop Doing
Things I Could Never Do
Things I'd Change
Things I Do Every Day
Things I Do That Don't Involve the Internet
Things I Know About Love
Things I Learned the Hard Way
Things I Love About Winter/Spring/Summer/Fall
Things I'm Good At
Things I'm Sorry For
Things I Need Forgiveness For
Things I Thought I Could Never Do and Then Did
Things I've Stopped Doing
Things I Was Wrong About
Things I Wish I Could Get Paid to Do
Things I Wish I Had the Guts to Say
Things I Wish You Would Do
Things That Are Fun to Touch
Things That Need Ending
Things That Need Tending
Things That Scare Me
Things That Scared Me as a Child
Things That Should Be Obvious
Things They Don't Teach in School
Things to Do with Someone I Love
Things You Should Know About Girls/Guys

Things We Don't Talk About
Those I've Loved
Times I Left
Times I Stayed
Times I Was Afraid
Times I Was Stuck
Toys I've Known
Transitions
Trees I've Known
Ways I Know I'm Alive
Weapons of Defense
Wishes

Everything I Know Abouts

Set the timer for six minutes and write everything you know about . . .

Babysitters
Bad roads
Basements
Being a man
Being a woman
Being brave
Being born
Carpeting
Change
Charity
Charm
Cheating
Cheese
Children
Creeps
Dolls

Ducks
Dusk
Electricity
Falling
Fashion
Fighting
Freedom
Funerals
Getting older
Getting started
Gingham
Ghosts
Goodness
Good taste
Grapes
Holiness
Hope
Houseguests
Ice cubes
Jury-rigging
Justice
Loneliness
Losers
Losing
Magic
Making time
Manners
Marriage
Marshmallows
Martyrs
Mean girls
Miracles

Mirrors
Mold
Monsters
Mustaches
My father/mother/brother/sister/grandparents
My feet
My hair
My neighbors
My nemesis
My voice
Need
Night
Nipples
Nurses
Pain
Parasites
Picnics
Playing
Pleasure
Principles
Promises
Prosperity
Rehabilitation
Riots
Romance
Runts
Ruts
Saints
Scarecrows
Shadows
Sissies
Slippage

Sluts
Sno-cones
Snooping
Static
Stealing
Strays
Striving
Taboos
Teenagers
The dark
The edge
Tradition
Traffic
Trying
Uniforms
Villains
Winners
Witches
Worms
Wrinkles

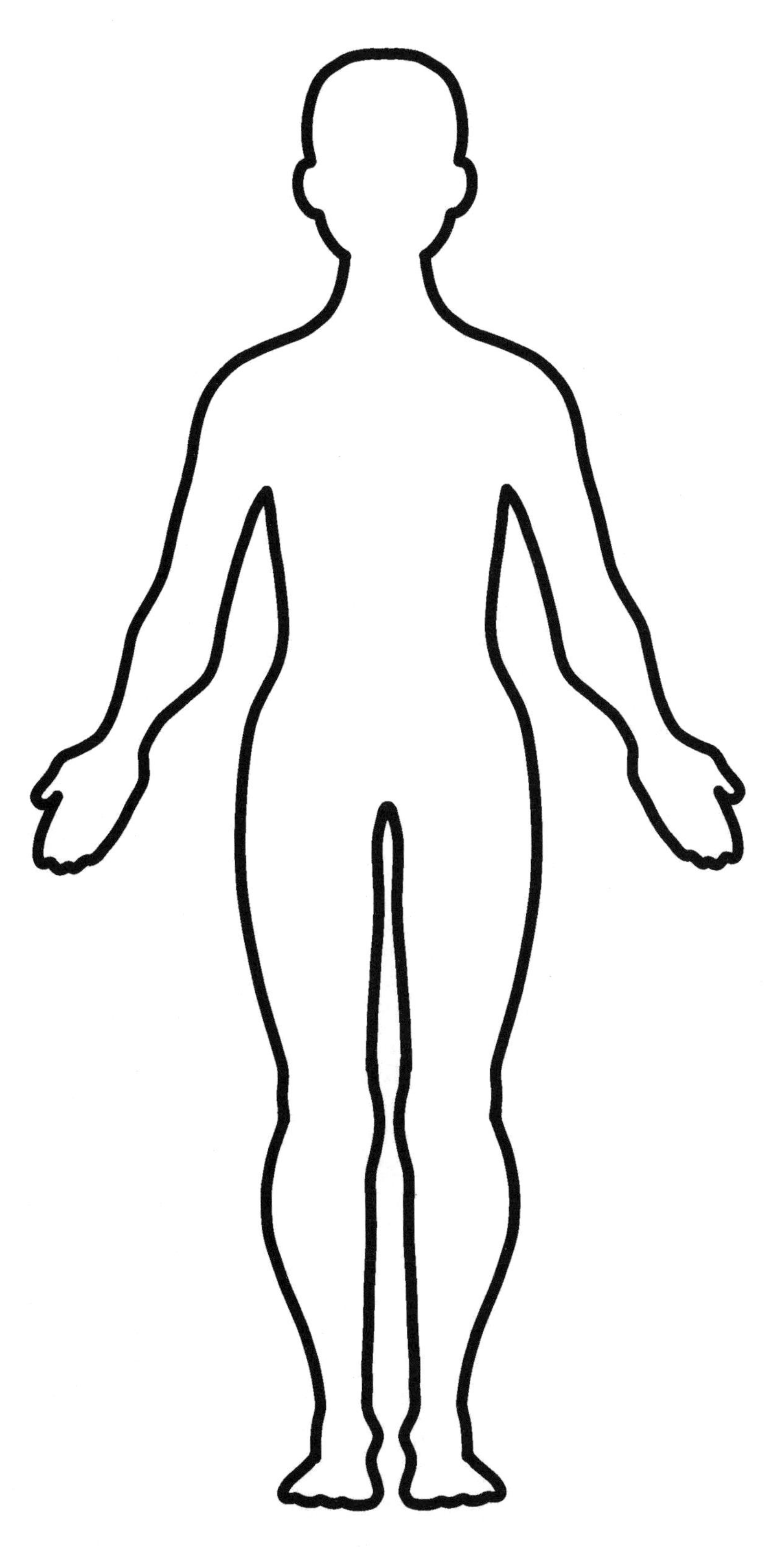

Acknowledgments

I owe a debt of gratitude to my acting and improvisation teachers for managing to fascinate me with the mysteries and mechanics of character and story, regardless of my as yet unacknowledged but wickedly potent fear and resistance.

And to the town of Ojai and its surprising and gorgeous inhabitants, thank you for making a place for me to create and learn and become larger than the sum of my parts. Thank you Theater 150 and its creators, supporters, and artists—you were the fire in which I was forged. Kira Ryder, of Lulu Bandha's Yoga Studio, your inspired teaching was a major influence on my own. And you hippies with whom I communed, thank you—despite those meetings, you were instrumental in reintroducing me to my part-wild nature.

Thank you, Zhena Muzyka, for creating such a soulful publishing company, for your unabashed championing of books and their authors, and for pairing me with editor Emily Heckman, who brilliantly guided me through the unlayering and revealing of this book.

To my writing group, thank you for your endless, loving integrity and for listening to these chapters so many, many times.

Thank you to my students and clients for bravely tending your part-wild natures and for inviting me into your processes.

Thank you, Dara Marks, my teaching partner, for matching my fervor for writing and for opening up so much new territory for exploration.

Most importantly of all, thank you, Mom, for never being the slightest bit thrown when I turned out to be such a strange child, for encouraging a certain level of feral behavior, and for never insisting that I have a Plan B.

About the Author

Deb Norton is a writing coach for screenwriters, novelists, and nonfiction writers. She leads writing workshops internationally, is a master teacher at Hedgebrook, and teaches immersive retreats in story structure and archetype. After graduating from the master of acting program at the American Conservatory Theater in San Francisco, she spent an eventful ten years dutifully pursuing her acting career before her desire for a deeper connection to Story led her to pen her own plays and screenplays. Her full-length play, *The Whole Banana*, has been optioned for a movie. She lives in the Northern Sierra Mountains in California.